FROM KNOWLEDGE TO INFLUENCE

The Credible Leader's Playbook

GEORGE J. McLEAN

"Any fool can see what is directly in front of them, but only a true leader has the vision to see around corners."
— Dr. George J. McLean

Copyright © 2025 Powerhouse Leadership Press.

All rights reserved.
No part of this book may be reproduced or transmitted in any form or by any means without written permission from the author.

ISBN 979-8-218-85257-3

Printed in the United States of America

DEDICATION

To the mentors and leaders, both formal and informal, whose guidance and example have shaped my growth. Your insight and support have made a lasting impact on this journey.

To my family, whose strength, love, and unwavering support have given me the resilience to persevere and the confidence to keep moving forward.

And to my team and family in Miami, thank you for your partnership, encouragement, and support. Your presence has brought meaning and momentum to this work.

This book reflects the people who have walked alongside me and influenced every step.

"If your actions inspire others to dream more, learn more, do more, and become more, you are a leader."
— John Quincy Adams

TABLE OF CONTENTS

Dedication v
Preface ix
Acknowledgments x
Opening Story xi

PART I
PLANTING THE SEEDS OF INFLUENCE

CHAPTER 1
    Perseverance as a Strategic Asset 1

CHAPTER 2
    Redefining Thought Leadership in the Modern Era 11

CHAPTER 3
    From Scholarship to Strategy 23

PART II
FROM KNOWLEDGE TO INFLUENCE

CHAPTER 4
    Building Influence through Credibility and Consistency 37

CHAPTER 5
    The Innovation Imperative 55

CHAPTER 6
    Navigating Disruption with Confidence 69

PART III
LEADING FROM WITHIN

CHAPTER 7
Storytelling as a Leadership Tool 91

CHAPTER 8
Leveraging Networks and Collaboration 101

CHAPTER 9
Ethical Influence in a Complex World 113

CHAPTER 10
Shaping the Future: A Thought Leader's Legacy 123

Conclusion 131
Author's Note 132
About the Author 133

PREFACE

This book was not created overnight; it is the culmination of more than fifteen years of experience, education, and purposeful growth in the field of business and leadership. I envisioned and designed this text as a practical resource for emerging and aspiring leaders who are ready to elevate their thinking, refine their craft, and succeed within their respective industries.

Throughout my career, I have drawn on the lessons of mentors, the challenges of complex environments, and the insights gained from both scholarship and real-world practice. These experiences have shaped my perspectives on credibility, influence, and the responsibility that modern leaders carry. The concepts in this book are not theoretical; they are grounded in lived experience, applied knowledge, and a commitment to helping others unlock their potential.

My hope is that these chapters serve as a guide, driving force, and companion on your leadership journey. Whether you are navigating your first professional role or driving strategic initiatives at a higher level, the principles shared here are designed to support your growth, strengthen your decision-making, and empower you to lead with intention, clarity, and confidence.

Thank you for allowing me to share this journey with you. May this book inspire you to pursue excellence, embrace innovation, and shape your own path with purpose and integrity.

— Dr. George J. Mclean

ACKNOWLEDGMENTS

I want to thank my friends and family, whose support has carried me through every personal and professional pursuit. Your encouragement has given me the strength to grow, evolve, and continue striving for excellence.

To my work family, I cannot thank you enough. You have supported me, challenged me, and stood alongside me through every season of my journey. Your unwavering belief in my potential has fueled my relentless pursuit of growth, and I am deeply grateful for the trust, collaboration, and inspiration each of you has given me.

A personal thank you to Alejandra Argudin, whose leadership, example, and commitment to excellence continue to inspire me. Your guidance has shaped the way I think about service, integrity, and the responsibilities of leadership.

And to Angel Diaz, Angela Sanchez and Victor Rosario, thank you for your mentorship, encouragement, and opportunities to learn, grow, and contribute at a higher level. Your confidence in my work has pushed me to reach beyond my comfort zone and broaden my impact.

This book reflects the people who poured into me, pushed me, and helped shape who I am today. Thank you for walking this path with me and for being part of the story behind these pages.

> *"From everyone who has been given much, much will be demanded; and from the one who has been entrusted with much, much more will be asked."*
> *— Luke 12:48*

OPENING STORY

Perseverance is a term we've heard throughout our lives, often in the context of sports, academics, and professional achievements. Yet, few pause to consider its true meaning, or how it shapes decision-making, resilience under pressure, and the ability to navigate challenges in pursuit of long-term goals. At its core, perseverance is the continued effort to achieve a goal, even when the journey is difficult or takes a long time. But how does this determination take shape? And what transforms such an abstract concept into a tangible asset that strengthens our lives, careers, and overall well-being? These are the questions that led me to explore perseverance, not simply as a personal value, but as a strategic asset in life.

Before we explore the ideology of perseverance, I want to share its roots in my life and how it has shaped me. Moving to Miami as a child meant entering a world that was both exciting and intimidating. On my first day at my new school, I stepped off the bus, a lanky six-foot-two teenager with a country accent from Atlanta, Georgia. Within minutes, I was met with two questions that seemed to define me from that moment onward: "Do you play basketball?" and "Where are you from?" After I answered both, the other kids quickly lost interest. Being an introvert by nature also didn't help me make friends, and for a while, I found myself on the outside, looking in.

Miami felt like another world. The pace was faster, the energy more intense, and within my first few weeks, I found myself surrounded by different languages, including Spanish, Creole, and Portuguese, none of which I spoke or understood natively. It was a complete culture shock, and I struggled to find my place in a city that seemed to run on a rhythm I didn't yet know how to dance to. Adapting to this new environment required more than just learning to fit in or keeping an open mind. It demanded a level of resilience and adaptability that I would only come to understand years later. It required the ability to navigate unfamiliar situations with confidence, to show up every day with the effort, energy, and attitude needed to overcome challenges. After noticing this, I was able to consistently put forth the effort necessary to overcome these challenges and make the lifelong friends that ultimately serve as the inspiration for this book.

These early years first introduced me to the concept of perseverance, showing me that progress often comes in small and often uncomfortable steps. I learned that perseverance goes beyond personal discipline; it is the driving force behind growth, achievement, and leadership.

PART I

PLANTING THE SEEDS OF INFLUENCE

Laying the Foundation for Thought Leadership

Chapter 1

Perseverance as a Strategic Asset

"Success is not final, failure is not fatal: It is the courage to continue that counts." – Winston Churchill

Perseverance is often an overlooked quality in leadership, recognized only in hindsight after a goal is achieved or a significant challenge is overcome. Yet, as many of us discover later in life, it is the foundation of the journey itself. More than just a personality trait, perseverance is an intrinsic value that provides a competitive edge in life. At this point, it becomes a strategic asset that we rely on in times of adversity. This is not uncommon. History has repeatedly shown us examples where perseverance was the key to success for many of society's most influential leaders.

For example, Martin Luther King Jr., a Civil Rights leader who spent 13 years fighting for racial equality, social justice, and economic fairness, first emerged as a prominent figure in 1955. However, his place on the national stage was cemented in 1963 with his iconic "I Have a Dream" speech, delivered after years of relentless advocacy, organizing, and personal sacrifice. His unwavering commitment, despite threats, imprisonment, and constant opposition, illustrates that perseverance is not merely enduring hardship. It is the ability to stay committed to a vision, adapt strategies when necessary, and continue pressing forward until that vision is realized.

This was not limited to civil rights leaders. In the business world, Steve Jobs personified the true meaning of perseverance, overcoming significant challenges throughout his career. After being ousted from Apple, the company he co-founded, Jobs could have walked away from the tech industry altogether. Instead, he poured his energy into new ventures, including Pixar and NeXT, both of which would go on to revolutionize their respective fields. When he eventually returned to Apple, he brought with him a renewed vision, leading the company through one of the most remarkable corporate turnarounds in history. His story demonstrates that perseverance in business is not just about weathering setbacks, it is about using those moments as defining elements for reinvention and greater success.

In science, one of the greatest examples of perseverance is Thomas Edison, the inventor of the practical incandescent light bulb. Edison's path to success was anything but straightforward. He reportedly conducted over 2,700 experiments before achieving a working design in 1879. Each failure was not a setback but a lesson, refining his approach and bringing him closer to his goal. His relentless determination is evidence of how perseverance enables individuals to overcome obstacles and ultimately accomplish their life's ambitions.

After reflecting on all these examples, I quickly began evaluating the circumstances that made them successful in their own right and noticed one underlying principle across all the examples. Yes! You guessed it: perseverance. Each of these leaders not only demonstrated foresight, but they also demonstrated a high level of dedication to their cause and a willingness to make personal sacrifices that ultimately led to their extraordinary accomplishments in history.

Then it dawned on me that this was not an anomaly, and these same characteristics serve modern-day leaders as a strategic asset, enabling them to remain resilient in a complex world that is constantly changing and evolving. However, before I could fully explain the power of perseverance and its connection to successful leadership, I had to explore the underlying principles that serve as its foundation.

The Underlying Principles of Perseverance

Resilience

Resilience is the ability to quickly bounce back from challenges, adapt to change, and recover from setbacks and adversity. It goes beyond an unwavering commitment to reach a goal; it encompasses the flexibility to shift perspectives and reframe how we view obstacles. Resilience is not about ignoring adversity, but about learning to harness it as an enabler for growth.

This was one of the most valuable lessons I learned in my professional career, navigating the world of corporate America. I was daily confronted with the pressures of meeting tight project deadlines, navigating organizational politics, and delivering innovative solutions that aligned with the CEO's vision. These experiences taught me that success depended not just on skill or determination, but on the ability to recover quickly, remain adaptable, and continue moving forward even when the circumstances felt overwhelming.

That is where I first learned to weaponize the three Cs of resilience, transforming them into a tool that allowed me to prevail in the face of adversity and grow into a leader in my field.

The first C is *Challenges*. We all face challenges in our personal and professional lives, but what makes us resilient is not the absence of obstacles; it is our perspective. Resilient people shift to a growth mindset, choosing to see adversity as a learning opportunity rather than an immovable barrier. This reframing not only helps us push through difficulties but also sharpens our ability to innovate and adapt.

The second C is *Control*. Every one of us has an inner desire to control outcomes, especially in situations where we feel powerless. The difference between the average person and a resilient leader lies in how they define control in the context of adversity. Early in my professional career, I learned that my trajectory changed dramatically when I stopped dwelling on factors outside my control and, instead, focused on what I could influence. This shift freed up time, energy, and mental capacity to direct my efforts toward what truly mattered: delivering results and winning!

The final C is *Commitment*. This pillar of resilience is the one I value most, and it has had the greatest impact on my life. Commitment has always stood out to me because it does not matter what degree you hold or what professional title you carry. At some point, every one of us encounters a situation that demands an extraordinary level of commitment to succeed. It is in these moments that true resilience is revealed, not by talent or credentials alone, but by the willingness to stay engaged, push forward, and refuse to give up.

These three Cs are the key elements that make resilience such a powerful tool. As I reflect on my own journey and study the paths of influential leaders today, I quickly recognize how interconnected they are. But resilience alone does not complete the foundation of perseverance. The leaders were not only resilient, but they were also adaptable. They thrived by adjusting to shifting political, social, and business landscapes, transforming uncertainty into opportunity. It was this adaptability, combined with their resilience, that allowed them to evolve and ultimately become the successful leaders history remembers.

Adaptability

I remember early in my career hearing my CEO preach about the importance of being adaptable in a constantly changing business environment. At the time, I nodded along, but I never truly understood what he meant until the day I was challenged with a lateral position change. I did not fully grasp the reasoning behind it, and part of me questioned if it was really a step forward. I was anxious, uncertain, and full of doubt. But then, I remembered the key lesson of adaptability. Instead of resisting the change, I decided to shift my mindset. I chose to put my best foot forward, embrace the opportunity, and adjust to the new role requirements. That decision became a turning point in how I viewed my career.

Adaptability, at its core, is about adjusting to new conditions, being flexible, and learning new skills. It is not about having all the answers; it is about being willing to grow into them. For leaders, adaptability becomes the crux of emerging as change agents. It means *shifting perspective*, *preparing for the unexpected*, and *staying persistent* in the face of uncertainty. The ability to adapt is what separates leaders who merely survive change from those who use it as a platform to lead transformation.

This change in my position required me to strategically shift my perspective and open my eyes to a broader view of my career trajectory. Before the move, I was simply a leader impacting a small division of the organization and did not yet see the larger vision of my CEO. However, once I shifted my perspective, my eyes were opened. I began to see the "whole field," understanding exactly where my talents were needed to help push the entire organization forward. That moment became a turning point in my career, a moment of choice where I could either push forward or give up. And you guessed it: I pushed forward. Not only did I push forward, but I also began preparing for the future and the unexpected, embracing adaptability as a core principle of my leadership journey.

Preparing for the future was an ideal that, before this transition, I rarely considered an essential element of perseverance. It was not due to a lack of focus on professional development. I have always been a lifelong student, eager to learn and pursue opportunities. Rather, it was a lack of intentional focus when it came to preparing for both my personal and professional goals.

When reflecting on the pillar of **Preparation**, I am often reminded of the old saying, *"Jack of all trades, master of none."* That phrase described exactly how my preparation had been taking shape, broad but unfocused, scattered rather than strategic.

True preparation is more than accumulating knowledge; it is about being proactive and deliberate. It requires continuous learning, building contingency plans, and taking strategic steps toward both personal and professional growth. Preparation is the discipline of positioning oneself not just for the challenges of today, but for the opportunities of tomorrow.

Once you finally shift your perspective on preparation, the next step is becoming obsessively persistent in the pursuit of your goals. We can have all the tools in the world, but the real test of a person is revealed in the face of adversity. This is where all the principles come together to build the framework for adaptability.

This lesson became real to me when I transitioned into a new position and, for the first time, began to lose motivation for what I thought was my ultimate career goal. I had been preparing for a path toward executive leadership, but after the transition, I realized my preparation had been too broad and unfocused. That lack of clarity weakened the pursuit of my goals, forcing me to confront the gaps in my professional development.

This was my turning point. I had to decide whether I would remain discouraged or rise with renewed determination. I chose persistence. I became more disciplined, built momentum, and refused to let obstacles or unforeseen events throw me off course. From that point on, persistence was no longer just a nice-to-have quality; it became the fuel that kept me advancing on my professional journey, no matter the setbacks.

Discipline

To consistently practice all these traits that make up perseverance in my daily life, I found that one final pillar was required: discipline. Discipline goes beyond simply showing up every day. It is the practice of consistently putting forth effort to achieve your goals, even on the days when you do not want to or when motivation is low. True discipline is about showing up anyway, maintaining focus, and delivering your best effort regardless of how you feel. This is one of the final lessons I learned early in my professional career as a junior manager. I remember starting my management career as a rambunctious 22-year-old, fresh out of college, with more enthusiasm than experience. At that point, the only leadership role I had held was serving as president of the FIU chapter of the NAACP, an on-campus civil rights organization with just eight members, including myself, who were determined to create a better future for our college.

This was the moment I began to recognize the importance of practicing discipline as a pillar of success for my professional journey. Managing a small group of college students had already shown me the value of resilience and adaptability, but discipline was not yet in my vocabulary. I truly did not have a clear understanding of what the word meant, how to apply it, or how it could shape my growth.

That became evident when I held my first team meeting after being promoted to branch manager. I remember it like it was yesterday. This was a major step up from my college leadership role. Now I had the power and responsibility of guiding the careers of others, making decisions that could have a lasting impact on my team. My palms were sweaty, my heart was racing, and when I finally spoke, my voice lacked confidence. My team remained quiet, unsure how to respond to my uncertainty.

As I went through the checklist in my head, I realized I had covered resilience and adaptability, but something was missing. That was my *aha* moment. I had no discipline. I was showing up, but I was not fully prepared. I lacked the structure, the consistency, and the intentional focus needed to lead with confidence. That realization became the starting point for my growth, showing me that discipline was the glue that held all the other qualities together and formed the foundation of perseverance. Perseverance requires consistent effort, even when motivation fades. Discipline turns intention into habit, ensuring progress is made daily, whether through study, practice, or incremental decision-making.

This was not something I realized overnight; it took more than 15 years of experiences, lessons, and reflection before I could finally articulate these ideas and put pen to paper to write this book. In exploring these lessons, I came to understand that perseverance is more than just a leadership quality; it is a mindset, a discipline, and a lifelong practice that shapes every aspect of personal and professional success. And my hope is that as you read the remainder of this book, you gain a genuine understanding of the role perseverance plays in leadership and why it is a strategic asset that can help you achieve what may seem like insurmountable goals.

Reflecting on these experiences, I see the critical role that resilience, adaptability, and discipline play in practicing perseverance. When we step back and look at history's most influential leaders, a pattern emerges—a common denominator, a kind of 'secret sauce' that unites them all. As we continue exploring perseverance, you'll see that the lessons shared here did not emerge from one defining moment but evolved through years of growth and experience. This journey includes earning my doctorate in business administration, serving as a civic leader, teaching as a professor, consulting across industries, and advising at the executive level. I will use these experiences to highlight and provide learning moments that demonstrate how perseverance is built and applied.

This book is my attempt to galvanize the importance of perseverance in thought leadership. In the chapters ahead, we will explore how these practices can help you reimagine your personal leadership style and position yourself as a thought leader in your industry. That is the goal. My hope is that by reading this text, your view of perseverance will shift, and you will begin to see it as a strategic asset in your life. Perseverance is about more than just surviving hard moments; it is about becoming stronger, more capable, and better prepared for the opportunities that lie ahead.

Chapter 2

Redefining Thought Leadership in the Modern Era

"People don't buy what you do; they buy why you do it."
– Simon Sinek

Thought leadership in the modern era is often overlooked or underappreciated by industry professionals. Many leaders ask themselves: What exactly is thought leadership? How can I practice it consistently? Why should I invest my time in it if I am already established in my field? These are common and valid questions, yet they reveal a misunderstanding of the true value thought leadership brings to personal growth, professional credibility, and long-term influence.

In its simplest form, thought leadership is the expression of ideas that demonstrate expertise in a particular field, area, or topic. But is it really that simple? Across industries, both private and public, leaders often debate its value. For some, thought leadership is treated as a formality—a box to check to maintain visibility. I would argue, however, that it is more than that. Thought leadership is a strategic asset that shapes influence, drives innovation, and distinguishes leaders who merely participate in their industry from those who define it.

I came to understand the value of thought leadership later in my career, when I first created a platform to share my personal insights and professional lessons. That experience showed me that thought leadership had evolved far beyond its original meaning and was now a powerful way to build trust and credibility in the digital era. But before we discuss the implications that digital platforms have on thought leadership, we must first evaluate how they shape and impact our own unique leadership styles in practice.

Historically, leadership was viewed primarily as a matter of expertise. A leader's value was measured by technical knowledge, subject-matter authority, credentials, and the ability to make sound decisions. Over time, this view of leadership has dramatically changed and evolved. It has shifted from a purely technical focus to a broader, more strategic approach that values not only expertise, but also empathy, laying the foundation for both modern thought leadership and the rise of relational leadership in the business environment.

As a mid-level professional, I was dismayed when I finally began to understand the interplay between thought leadership and relational leadership, a topic that is rarely discussed. How do these two influence one another? Are they equally important? And how should they shape my own view of leadership? These were some of the questions that raced through my mind when I was first assigned to a leadership position in corporate America.

Being a leader in corporate America was very different from working as a blue-collar retail supervisor. In retail, I supervised people, but in truth, I merely managed them. I told them what to do and when to do it, and followed up to make sure it was done. Looking back on it now, I realize I was shamefully a disciplinarian at heart. With the benefit of now of 18 years of experience and 15 years of studying business management and leadership, I can now admit that I was doing it all wrong. Leadership is not about control or discipline alone; it is about influence, inspiration, and the ability to bring out the best in others.

This was where I first discovered the power of relational leadership and how it could serve as a precursor to thought leadership. *Relational leadership is a human-centered, collaborative approach that emphasizes building trust-based relationships to foster inclusivity, achieve shared goals, and create positive change.* This was very different from the traditional leadership I had practiced in the past, which depended strictly on power and control. Over time, I began to shift my priorities toward creating a psychologically safe environment where my team members felt valued, heard, and empowered to contribute their diverse perspectives during our weekly meetings. This change became the strategic driver for my transition into modern thought leadership, and it was one of the ways I began to define myself as a leader in my industry and community.

As my leadership style evolved, I felt increasingly compelled to share my findings with others in my industry, and before long, I found myself participating in my first local conference. I remember it like it was yesterday. Shortly after attending, I was invited to serve on the educational committee and tasked with organizing a mid-year session on leadership. This was where it all began. At the time, I was a manager of operations with very little experience in the industry, yet there I was, confidently interjecting my opinions about 'how to be a good leader' and even directing seasoned professionals on what I wanted them to cover in their sessions. The surprising part was that they listened to me, even though I was a young professional with big ambitions trying to change the way things were done in an industry that, for the most part, was highly resistant to change.

This was the first major learning lesson of my professional career: to be bold, confident, and never waver from your ideas or vision. Soon after this event, I was approached to participate in my first media campaign, promoting an industry certification, which required me to create a social media video that would be shared across the industry. The funny part is that, at the time, I was still unaware that I was slowly becoming a thought leader in my field. But after completing the campaign, naively at first, I began to realize the power that digital platforms hold in shaping and amplifying this concept of thought leadership.

At the time of publishing this book, digital platforms like Instagram, Facebook, LinkedIn, and YouTube were the primary channels for sharing ideas and insights. These platforms allow you to reach a diverse audience with the press of a button. At the time, I had no idea how powerful these tools would become or the impact they would ultimately have on my professional career. Over the next eight years, I came to understand how they had evolved into visibility engines that drive influence, credibility, and connection in the modern era. Although it may seem that simple, and at first, I believed it was, I later learned there were other important considerations I had to make to use these platforms effectively as a leader in my industry.

It was more than just sharing insights. It grew bigger than that. The more opportunities I gained, the more I began to feel a yawning sense that something was missing or not fully aligning within myself. That was when it hit me: I needed to connect the work I was doing with my personal brand and mission by taking a more focused approach. I had to narrow in on my expertise, becoming a subject matter expert in my field. This shift allowed me not only to share knowledge, but also to contribute to the field by creating it. Yet, this realization created more questions than answers, because at the time, I had no clear idea how to even begin. How do I achieve this thing called alignment? Why does it even matter? Why can't I simply speak from the heart and share my stories?

Alignment, in the general sense, means consistently expressing your core values and unique perspective in a way that is authentic, builds trust, and drives impact. This was it. Learning to align my efforts in a coordinated way would help me build the credibility I needed to move to the next level. At that time, I was participating in smaller local conferences and individual social campaigns, but I never built momentum. I would be asked to contribute here and there, yet nothing ever felt consistent. This was the moment in my career when I began to focus on alignment as a way to elevate my personal brand.

The first step was to clarify my core mission. I had to decide what I honestly wanted to accomplish. I did this by asking myself some hard questions: Why am I doing this? What do I want to achieve by sharing these insights? Am I being cynical in my efforts, or are these genuine attempts at altruism? Let's just say this was an eye-opening exercise that I encourage all professionals to undertake at some point in their careers. The findings were surprising, to say the least.

I realized that many of my earlier attempts at sharing insights were derived from the idea that "my way was the only way" and that everyone else was doing it wrong. But after completing this exercise, I recognized that this was never my intention. What I wanted was to share a different perspective—insights that had worked for me and might one day help others. It became one of the most valuable lessons of my journey. It forced me to confront a difficult question: how had I strayed so far from my original mission, and how could I get back on track? More importantly, how could I help others stay aligned with their own mission? This soon became my focus.

To answer these questions, we must look closely at how many of us unconsciously fall into this pitfall. That is where I discovered that our internal biases ultimately shape how we view the world. Through my research, I found it was often a combination of cognitive biases, emotional needs, and psychological factors. These included the belief that we have complete information (even when we do not), confirmation bias, emotional attachment to our existing beliefs, the desire to protect a fragile ego, and the false-consensus effect, which leads us to overestimate how much others agree with us.

Boom! That is when it hit me! These were the reasons I strayed from my original mission and became the cynical version of myself at that time. Instead of continuing to protect my ego, I decided it was time to move forward and embrace risk to get back on track. This shift put me in a position to help others while also reaching the level of self-fulfillment I had been seeking all my life.

Now that I understood how I had drifted off course, I knew I needed to shift my focus to realignment, getting back on track, and then helping others follow my lead. I did this by aligning my brand with my mission. At the time, my personal brand was something I had largely taken for granted, but as my professional career progressed, I quickly learned to appreciate and value its importance. The biggest challenge I faced was removing all the noise and defining my brand, deciphering what I wanted it to mean to others. When people hear the name, Dr. George McLean, what thoughts do I want to come to mind in the first 30 seconds? How do I want to be remembered? These are the very questions we all need to ask ourselves to define our personal brand and to determine the changes we must make to shape it into our vision.

The first step to answering these questions is to define your brand pillars. Professionally, personal brand pillars are the core values, skills, and actions that shape your identity and reputation. In simpler terms, think of it this way: if you asked someone to describe you in 30 seconds using verbs, what would you want them to say? Then ask yourself: do my actions truly support this description? If not, it may be time to establish new brand pillars and set goals that will help you reimagine your brand and align.

This was something I knew I had to complete, especially at this vulnerable stage in my career when I had only just discovered the very concept of a personal brand. And what I found was astonishing, to say the least. I asked several people what came to mind in the first 30 seconds when they heard my name, and guess what? It was nothing like what I had imagined. I thought I would hear words like Strategic Innovator, Civic Leader, Inspirational Leader, Disruptor, or even Community Leader. Instead, to my surprise, I heard words like manager, bossy, know-it-all, forceful, and aggressive.

This was the enlightening moment when it suddenly struck me that I needed to complete a brand realignment in order to reach my full potential. *Personal brand realignment is the strategic process of redefining your public identity so that it accurately reflects your current professional goals, core values, and the reputation you want to build.* But where do I start? How do I change their perspective? I had already written down what I wanted people to think, but how could I get them to think that? This was the point where I realized I needed to take a deeper look into my personal brand and create a concrete plan. After conducting some research, I discovered that I had already completed step number one inadvertently. I had identified what I wanted my brand to be and compared it to what it actually was in my industry. That was when I discovered the gap.

Recognizing the gap was one thing but closing it was another. This was where things became a little ambiguous, because I learned that addressing it required not only communicating my new brand but also living it authentically through my actions. How I chose to do this was entirely up to me, and one of the most important things I discovered is that there is no one-size-fits-all approach. If you were expecting me to tell you exactly how to do it, I am sorry to disappoint. What I can share is how I did it, and my hope is that it sparks the creativity you need to design a plan that works for redefining your own brand.

When I undertook this brand realignment midway through my career, I started by conducting an internal audit. I went back to the trusted individuals who had helped me answer my first question about perception. This time, I asked them why they felt that way and what I could potentially do to change their opinion. Of course, this was not a change that could happen overnight, but the first step was identifying where the problem lay. I was once again shocked when I finally received all the feedback. To sum it up in a few words, I was told that I came across as very forceful in meetings, that I did not always consider other perspectives, and that when I presented my ideas online or on digital platforms, they were not well received. I was also told that I lacked credibility and confidence when speaking because I often said, "this is what I think," instead of using data and my expertise to validate my perspective.

This had to change, and it had to change quickly. The first thing I did was put words into action by designing a plan to address these blind spots in every aspect of my life. I immediately began taking a "listening first" approach to meetings. Next, I began encouraging feedback as a regular part of our meetings, by making it a standing item on every agenda. Finally, I committed hours to studying behavioral research, which taught me how to inspire change rather than force it, ultimately helping me grow into a change agent within my organization.

Once the plan was in place, I had to do the hardest part: authentically living it day in and day out. If you are like me, you understand why I call this the hardest part. It takes time to build new habits and stop slipping back into old ways. I noticed this problem right away. As quickly as I created the plan, I found myself slipping back into old behaviors. Soon, I began hearing feedback and quiet comments like, "I guess the old George is back," which was extremely alarming.

But this became a point of growth for me, and hopefully for you as well. I had to accept that I am not perfect, and that chasing perfection only leads to disappointment. What leads to change is consistency. Seeking consistency allows for steady growth and meaningful transformation, which is a realistic and achievable goal. That is how I learned to live my new brand authentically. As John C. Maxwell reminds us, *"Small disciplines repeated with consistency everyday lead to great achievements gained slowly over time."*

Once I began living my brand authentically, I finally started to see the fruits of my labor reflected in follow-up conversations with my peers. This was the moment when the change I had been striving for came into focus, and my influence began to expand across the industry. I was evolving into the leader I had always wanted to be, but one question remained: what makes someone influential? I had learned how to share my ideas and insights, but how could I translate that into influence? Put more simply, how do you really influence someone? Sharing ideas and insights is valuable, but the real work lies in inspiring change and action in others.

That realization forced me to rethink what true influence really meant. The idea was not foreign to me, but it was something I often overlooked. Previously, I focused on inspiring change and showing people what was possible, but that alone was not enough. It was not yielding the results I wanted. I would write an article or give a speech, and while people left motivated, very few acted on the information I shared. That was when I realized the difference between inspiring and influencing. Inspiration sparks motivation, but influence drives action. What I wanted was not just to inspire, but to influence real behavioral change.

But how do you do this? Simple: change the way you think. For me, it meant consistently sharing original and valuable insights, building trust through authenticity, and demonstrating expertise in my field. Tying these three concepts together into what I call the "trifecta" became paramount in my transition into an influential thought leader in my industry. I had finally found the formula for growth that would help me become the leader I had always strived to be in my community and industry. The time was here, but first I had to understand how to put each of these pillars into action in my daily life. Even more importantly, I had to grasp the true significance of each one.

This was challenging at first, but not impossible. I had been sharing what I thought were original and valuable insights for years, but I was still not considered influential. For the longest time, I had no idea why or what I was missing. Then it finally hit me. The ideas and insights I was contributing and labeling as "original" were not original at all. They were simply regurgitated information I had learned or read somewhere along the way in my career. This was a latent habit formed in college that followed me throughout my professional career. To fix this, I became a deep researcher, learning how to integrate both my academic knowledge and professional experience into practical lessons. This became the turning point that increased my influence in the industry.

Secondly, I had to begin building trust by using authenticity as a tool. Learning to apply this concept strategically in my professional career became a necessary step in facilitating the transition. I had to learn to communicate in a genuine and transparent way that created a safe space where others felt comfortable opening up, sharing their vulnerabilities, and being themselves. This was the foundation of psychological safety, and it became essential to my growth as a leader. It stood in sharp contrast to my previous communication style, which had failed me for years. This is where I learned that authenticity builds trust, and trust, in turn, builds influence.

To bring this all together, I had to demonstrate my expertise in the field to build credibility. That was when I realized that depth, not breadth, is what earns real influence. It became clear that I had spread myself too thin and lacked focus in any one area, which meant I could not truly be considered a subject matter expert. To address this, I went back to my roots and focused on strategic advising in policy and performance. I immersed myself in reading, blogging, and digesting everything I could find on emerging industry trends and news. After straying from my original path, I knew I had to re-benchmark myself against the industry I loved before I could continue creating and leading within it.

Discovering these pillars solidified my belief that thought leadership does not occur in a vacuum. It is driven by vision, not volume. That understanding shifted how I approached leadership in both my work and relationships . I came to realize that gaining influence stems from clarity of purpose and the ability to provide consistent value. In essence, thought leaders shape cultures rather than follow trends by reframing existing knowledge into fresh insight for the industry. This became my goal and mastering it gave me the power to emerge as an influential leader. It was what I had been chasing for years, and now, I finally had the knowledge and understanding to make it a reality and lead with impact.

Chapter 3

From Scholarship to Strategy

"Knowledge without application is meaningless." – Thomas Edison

This was the turning point in my career. I knew it was time to put the knowledge I had gained to work. I had spent the last couple of years researching theories and implementing tactics in my professional life to facilitate this transition. At this stage, it was no longer about simply learning; it was about moving into institutional practice and applying those lessons to create a competitive advantage. As a mid-career professional, I quickly realized this meant transforming information into unique insights. I needed to make the transition from scholarship to strategy.

The first thing I did was adapt the theories to my specific use case. In a business context, I would call it tailoring them to my professional needs, but from an academic perspective, it was simply about applying them to my situation. This became a pivotal aspect of designing strategies that could achieve the outcomes I wanted. In my early thought leadership days, before becoming an author, I had to learn how to transform these theories and lessons into actionable strategies that addressed real-world problems.

That was when I discovered it. This was the reason people would care about what I had to say. This is what is called developing a "so what" narrative, which, in simple terms, means explaining why what you are saying matters and why others should care. It is one thing to say that "AI is the future," but it is another to explain the implications AI will have on a multigenerational workforce and how to address the challenges that will come with this shift over the next ten years. By doing this, we move beyond simply restating facts and, instead, weave together a compelling narrative about the direction of the industry and the solutions needed to address its most complex problems.

We finally began using research and theories to solve real-world problems. This was where things became interesting, because I could highlight challenges and pain points that I genuinely believed in and that people truly faced in their daily lives. It was at this point that I first began to feel relevant in the industry, recognizing that I could use the platform I had established to become a change maker. To me, this meant I was finally in control. Instead of simply following industry trends, I could begin shaping and creating them. I was now in the driver's seat.

The first step was identifying a compelling problem that was big enough to matter but focused enough to be solved. At the time, that problem was figuring out how companies could adapt to the widespread use of Artificial Intelligence in our industry. This was an area where I had firsthand experience. Not only had I written my doctoral dissertation on technology acceptance in the multigenerational workforce, but I had also spent several years as a strategic innovator in my role as a Senior Business Analyst, developing solutions to the same challenge. Together, this experience became my ticket to becoming a subject matter expert, qualifying me to speak on the topic and propose solutions to peers across the industry.

One of the most natural aspects of this approach was that I could share not only the solutions, but also the mistakes I had made along the way. This honesty became critical when discussing AI adoption in our industry, because I had made plenty of mistakes before discovering the strategies that worked.

At a local industry conference, I shared one such example from earlier in my career. A team I worked with wanted to accelerate digital transformation, so we deployed an internal ChatGPT system to improve workflows and decision-making. This was a huge mistake. We assumed our staff already had the knowledge and skills to strategically leverage the tool. But instead of boosting productivity, the rollout created confusion, frustration, and resistance to change.

The lesson we learned was clear: technology adoption is not about the tool; it is about the people using it. We realized that before rolling out new systems, we needed to build digital literacy and provide structured training.

Once we shifted our focus toward upskilling the workforce and supporting them through the transition, adoption rates improved dramatically. What began as a failed experiment evolved into a strategy that positioned us for long-term success in the digital era.

However, strategy does not exist in a vacuum. It is continually shaped by external forces such as technological advances, market shifts, and cultural dynamics, and must be refined over time to remain effective. This is where the next concept comes into play; something called the "feedback loop." This concept is important because it establishes a continuous feedback cycle between theory and practice that drives personal growth, while also strengthening your thought leadership.

The feedback loop is a theory centered on self-reflection and experimentation. It represents a critical juncture in your life where you can transform daily experiences into concrete lessons that refine both your understanding and your capabilities. This is the stage where, as many say, the real magic happens in your thought leadership journey.

It is also the point where you can intentionally reflect by reviewing your own actions and judgment.

Pause and Reflect Exercise

Take a few minutes to write down your honest answers to the following questions. Use them to identify patterns in your behavior and opportunities for growth.

- What worked well? Why?
- Where did you face resistance? What could you have done differently?
- Did your actions align with your values and goals?

"Reflection without action is just a mirror, showing you who you are but never changing who you become." — Dr. George J. McLean

In this moment, I created an actionable adjustment plan that allowed me to make specific, incremental changes to my behavior and approach. For me, this meant sitting down to journal about my different engagements, reviewing past approaches, and refining them for future situations. During this process, I began noticing small subtleties that I wanted to change to enhance my impact. These were not major issues that stood out immediately, but minor nuances such as interrupting people, saying "um," or failing to make eye contact. Applying the feedback loop method helped me not only improve, but also become more consistent, ensuring that my growth was continuous rather than a one-time event.

This approach helped me bring to light small inaccuracies in my behavior, but I quickly realized that self-reflection alone was not enough. My feedback process was incomplete without input from others. It sounds obvious, but in practice, it was intimidating. Still, it became a recurring theme in my journey toward thought leadership: asking others for feedback and input to develop a sound plan of action.

It was time to share the ideas I had jotted down during my journaling exercises (Pause and Reflect Activity) with trusted friends and colleagues to gauge their reactions. By this stage of my career, seeking feedback had become the foundation of my growth.

After researching ways to do this without overwhelming others with random emails or phone calls, I discovered a wide range of methods used by some of the most effective thought leaders in America. While the list could easily fill an entire book, I want to highlight the top three approaches that worked for me and helped me gather the feedback I needed to refine my approach.

My Top Three Feedback Methods:

- Present a draft of a new idea to a trusted peer group.
- Write a blog post or social media update to invite public commentary.
- Host an informal "lunch and learn" session with close friends or colleagues to discuss a theory you are developing.

Hearing this feedback helped me shift from being defensive and guarded to adopting a growth mindset, where I began to treat feedback as valuable new data rather than personal criticism. But it was more than just hearing the feedback; I had to strategically listen to turn those words into action. Once they became actions, I then analyzed both quantitative metrics, such as likes and views, and qualitative feedback, such as comments and questions, to review my thought process and strengthen my influence. It was at this stage that I truly made the leap from theory to strategy, using my doctoral mindset to add depth and rigor to my strategic thinking.

"In thought leadership, words ignite action, and action leaves consequences that define your influence." — Dr. George J. McLean

When I began applying my refined theory back into practice, I quickly realized there were many considerations to keep in mind. I was working to fully understand and harness the power of thought leadership. These included conducting mini experiments, turning tension into innovation, and committing to becoming a lifelong learner. Each of these practices not only reshaped my perspective but also strengthened my influence. Once again, thought leadership does not exist in a vacuum. It develops over time and constantly evolves in response to environmental pressures.

But how do we do this? That was another tough question I had to address. When we take a pragmatic approach, the instinct is to simply choose the next step that sounds reasonable. However, it was not that simple. For this to work, I had to take an unconventional approach to implementing these strategies in the real world.

When I first began conducting mini experiments, it seemed intuitive to try different tactics and gauge my success by head-nods and kudos. But was that really success? In the context of thought leadership, unconventional approaches are defined as methods, strategies, or perspectives that deviate from traditional or widely accepted norms. They often involve creative or original ideas designed to solve problems or achieve goals in unique and impactful ways.

Applying this theory to solve our problems was an interesting exercise. When it came to conducting mini experiments, it was more than just relying on a traditional approach. I had to think outside the box and design new ways to get the results I desired. I did this by taking a few deliberate steps to accurately gauge the success of these new tactics. In developing my plan, I followed the adage: *"Keep It Simple, Stupid" (KISS)*. The simpler the design, the easier it was to track results, learn quickly, and make meaningful adjustments. This method proved successful, and I was able to quickly adapt it to the next steps in my journey.

Framework: Mini-Experiments (KISS Method)

- **Implement** – Keep the intervention simple and repeatable (e.g., A/B testing, role reversal).
- **Measure** – Select 2 - 3 signs of impact (such as engagement levels, actions taken, or follow-up activity).
- **Reflect & Adjust** – Review what worked, what surprised you, and what you would change if you repeated the experiment.

When I moved on to turning tensions into innovation, the transition felt much easier. The tensions I am referring to are the moments of feedback we receive from friends and colleagues that challenge our views and sometimes trigger defensiveness. Turning this into innovation means shifting our perspective, viewing adversity through the lens of curiosity, and reframing failure as an opportunity to grow and create.

Over time, I organized these insights into a simple framework that I still use today:

Framework: Turning Tension into Innovation

- **Pause** – Resist the instinct to react defensively. Take a moment to process the feedback or challenge.
- **Reframe** – Ask, *"What can I learn from this?"* or *"What opportunity does this challenge reveal?"*
- **Apply** – Test a new approach, idea, or behavior based on the insight gained.
- **Innovate** – Turn the lesson into a strategy or solution that creates value for yourself, your team, or your industry.

Lastly, I had to commit to the idea of becoming a lifelong learner. For years, I thought of myself as a student of my industry; someone who kept up with the latest trends. But when entering the big leagues of influencing others, I quickly learned it takes more. It was not enough to maintain the status quo. I needed to become a sophisticated leader in my own right, offering my industry new insights and perspectives from a qualified and credible source.

That realization led to another personal framework I use to guide my ongoing development:

Framework: The Lifelong Learning Loop

- **Curiosity** – Stay curious by asking new questions and identifying gaps in knowledge or practice.
- **Consume** – Read widely, not just within your field, but across disciplines to spark fresh ideas.
- **Create** – Turn what you've learned into insights, strategies, or practices that add value to others.
- **Cycle** – Repeat the process to continuously deepen your expertise and credibility over time.

Mini Case Study: The Turning Point

Before

I will never forget the moment after my second speaking engagement. I walked off the stage and realized something was off. During the Q&A, not a single hand went up. Afterward, maybe one or two people came up to me and politely said, "Thank you," and that was it. When I compared that to other speakers, the difference was glaring. Their Q&A sessions went long and people lined up for photos, exchanged emails, and set up follow-ups. None of that was happening for me. I knew right then I was missing something.

Application

That is when I started leaning into what I now call the Growth Toolbox. I went back and reflected on my talks deeply, journaled about what I thought went wrong, and asked myself some hard questions. Why should people care about what I am saying? How does this connect to what they are going through day to day? I also realized I was just sharing information instead of creating real insight. I began to push myself, not just to repeat things I had read, but to create new ideas that blended my research with my experiences.

After

Once I started doing that, the change came quickly. In just a few months, my Q&A sessions started filling with questions. People came up afterward, not only to thank me, but to ask for my slides, invite me to follow-ups, or even request collaborations. I went from barely being noticed to really connecting with my audience.

Lesson Learned

The Growth Toolbox is not a magic trick or something that works overnight. It took me time and a lot of refining before I started to see results. But once I stuck with it, it became one of the most valuable things I had ever applied in my career.

Elon Musk: Turning Tension into Innovation

This reminds me of one of the most influential leaders of our time, at least in my opinion. Who am I talking about? Elon Musk, the man who revolutionized space exploration and sustainable energy. When we review his journey, we notice plenty of common themes that show how this same framework applies to his rise as one of the most prominent thought leaders, so influential that even the President of the United States, Donald J. Trump, has acknowledged his impact.

When we apply this framework to study Musk's rise to prominence, we discover some serious commonalities. One of the keys to his success was being what I call a **strategic disruptor** in industries like space travel, electric vehicles, and solar energy. He consistently followed the path less traveled instead of relying on traditional business practices. Experimentation was one of the core staples of his success. As a true innovator, he created countless prototypes and failed even more times before finally achieving success with Tesla and the Falcon X rocket.

But that was not the only turning point in his long ascent to the top. He specialized in turning tension into innovation to achieve real results. Musk faced adversity that would have shattered the dreams of the average entrepreneur, and he excelled. This included pushbacks from governments, skepticism from Wall Street, and even criticism from his own employees. And it gets worse: at one point, both Tesla and SpaceX were on the brink of bankruptcy.

The fascinating part is that out of all this adversity emerged not just a car company, but an entire ecosystem: Tesla's Supercharger network, large-scale energy storage systems, reusable SpaceX rockets, and advances in autonomous driving. For Musk, tension became the inspiration source for industry-wide change. At his core, he has always been a lifelong learner, treating each failure not as an endpoint, but as a necessary step toward the next breakthrough.

Applying this framework to his journey shows us that leadership is not defined solely by bold visions, but by disciplined cycles of experimentation, reframing challenges, and continuously learning. This deliberate process of implementing simple experiments, turning tension into innovation, and committing to the lifelong learning loop is what allows Musk to move from idea to industry disruption in record time.

Leveraging Credibility and Rigor as Leadership Assets

When I reflected on the growth framework from a higher level, it started to illuminate something bigger than anything I had previously considered on this journey. This model is a prime example of resilience in action. When you think about the adversity and rigor required to rise to the top of any industry, we often assign credibility to those leaders, almost automatically. But what we rarely stop to consider is what it truly takes to be recognized as an expert in your field. This was the moment when all the dots connected for me, and I realized that credibility and rigor are not just outcomes of leadership; they are leadership assets.

Credibility and rigor are the natural byproducts of the Growth Framework, but they do not appear by accident. They can be cultivated and leveraged when a leader builds personal trust and consistently applies disciplined, evidence-based methods. When paired together, they transform ordinary experience into powerful, authentic thought leadership that not only inspires but also drives meaningful impact.

Personal credibility is the foundation, and rigor is the frame of thought leadership. Together, they strengthen your position as an industry leader and provide the stability needed to influence others with authenticity, authority, and lasting impact. When paired, they demonstrate integrity, showcase competence, and prove your ability to deliver results. This is a vital part of the transition from scholarship to strategy.

When applied to real-world scenarios, these principles elevate both solutions and decision-making. They become the engine that transforms generic ideas into meaningful, influential content. By taking a few deliberate steps, we can turn insight into action, action into credibility, and credibility into lasting influence. This requires mastering our niche, grounding ideas in evidence and data, challenging the status quo, and translating complex concepts into clear, accessible insights that resonate with a broad professional community. In the end, the lesson is simple: scholarship becomes strategy when it is applied with evidence, clarity, and relevance. Only then does knowledge move beyond theory to influence decisions and shape outcomes.

That philosophy became the foundation for the framework I use to move consistently from scholarship to strategy:

The Scholarship-to-Strategy Bridge

- **Ground** – Anchor your ideas in evidence, data, and credibility.
- **Translate** – Convert complex concepts into clear, accessible insights.
- **Apply** – Put knowledge into practice to solve meaningful problems.
- **Influence** – Turn applied knowledge into strategies that shape decisions and outcomes.

PART II
FROM KNOWLEDGE TO INFLUENCE

*We Are Now Credible
Thought Leaders*

The Path Ahead

In the first half of this book, we explored my personal journey from junior manager to senior executive, and how I learned to leverage thought leadership to build influence in my industry. Along the way, we examined the challenges I faced and how perseverance helped me overcome adversity. We also reviewed the strategies I used to rebrand my professional image, so it aligned with the values I represented. We shared the insights and lessons I gained throughout my career with power and influence.

This was the purpose of the chapter: to introduce you to the idea of perseverance and thought leadership in the modern era, and to show how these concepts can serve as strategic assets. Put simply, I wanted to share the value they added to my life in the hope that they will do the same for you, whether you are a junior manager just beginning your career or a senior executive striving to expand your influence, these lessons apply.

I recommend that you re-read the chapters with intention and use the frameworks to help you establish your platform. By making the effort to reflect and apply, you will uncover lessons unique to your own journey. The fact that you have read the first three chapters means you have already taken the first step in your personal pursuit of greatness.

I invite you to join me in Part II of this book as we continue down this rabbit hole together, exploring the power of perseverance and its role in shaping thought leadership in the modern era.

CHAPTER 4

BUILDING INFLUENCE THROUGH CREDIBILITY AND CONSISTENCY

"Trust is built with consistency." – Lincoln Chafee

One thing we have not yet explored is why consistency matters so much to visibility and trust in thought leadership. In today's world, where there are countless channels to communicate with your industry in real time, it begs the question: why is consistency so important in communication? This question reminds me of an old saying I used to hear from senior leadership: "You're only as good as your last meeting."

I never fully understood that phrase until I transitioned into executive leadership and faced the daily struggles of leading at a higher level. That was when it became clear to me that consistency is not about showing up for a single day or a single moment; it is about continually practicing the traits that define who you are as a leader. A consistent presence sends a strong signal of credibility and expertise. It is what differentiates a true thought leader from inconsistent or opportunistic voices that fade quickly from relevance.

This became evident when I finally earned the label of subject matter expert and began formally advising our executive leadership team on business matters. At the time, I was widely recognized and, for the most part, respected in my industry, which helped me secure the position.

However, I was aware of a major shortcoming: I lacked consistency. I often held back, driven by a fear of being perceived as condescending and by a lingering sense of imposter syndrome. The result was that, depending on the circumstances, people encountered different versions of me, and it was embarrassing. I vividly remember interviewing for my first executive role, when the hiring manager looked at me and said, "You are the man, but you are not the man today." That remark cut deep, pointing directly to my inconsistency and inadequacy in demonstrating the personal traits and confidence of a leader.

This experience sparked a fire in me. From that moment on, I dove into researching and studying the characteristics that could help me address this issue. What started as a personal mission quickly evolved into something bigger. Overtime, I developed a framework that not only helped me overcome my own inconsistency but also became a strategy I believe can help you too.

First, I had to align my words with my actions. I started here because it required a little practice but turned out to be one of the easiest fixes in the whole process. To do this, I made a short list of actions I wanted to change and set out the very next day to begin. To be transparent, most of these were behavioral and personality based.

I will take a moment to be vulnerable here and share an example of my starting point. Prepare yourself for the big reveal. It was simply "sitting up straight and being confident in meetings." Yes, that was it. I used to preach this as part of being a confident leader, yet I often struggled with it when speaking to CEOs or other executives. It was bad enough that I sometimes felt discouraged from sharing an idea at all. But I practiced, over and over, until I eventually achieved the goal.

However, changing this habit alone was not nearly enough to make it stick for the long term. As you have probably noticed by now,

I like to use sayings to drive points home and help you remember the key lessons. That's the professor in me. For this point, one of my favorites is, "Try it once, repeat it twice, but after three times, it becomes a habit."

This brings me to the second point: I needed to build micro-habits to turn my words into lasting actions that produced real results. That's where setting small, achievable goals came into play. For me, this meant reviewing my weekly schedule and setting an intention for each upcoming meeting, such as projecting confidence by consciously adjusting my posture. I wish I could say this came naturally, but the truth is it only became a habit through deliberate practice.

But this wasn't enough to successfully add the habit into my life. I was achieving small wins on a regular basis, but to gain true consistency, I needed more than just the wins themselves. I had to build a system to track those wins, so I could understand why I was gaining momentum and what behaviors were making the difference.

This sounded simple enough, right? Find a method to consistently document what I was doing and when. The key, however, was to make it as uncomplicated as possible, because we all know that if it is too cumbersome, it breeds inconsistency. Challenge accepted, and test passed. I simply created a note in my iPhone calendar. Yup, that simple, and I have no regrets about it.

Now, there are many ways to track these changes, such as journaling or using apps, but this was the system that worked for me. I encourage you to explore your own options and find something that feels simple, sustainable, and effective for you. As the saying goes, *"What gets measured, gets managed,"* and this was my time to manage my behaviors and finally make the changes I had always wanted in my life.

After I implemented this change, I had to finally embrace the last and final rule: the 80/20 rule. I had to adjust my expectations and aim for 80 percent consistency, finding a balance between discipline and happiness. This was critical because I realized if I was not happy, these new habits would never last.

Let me tell you a personal story to show you what I mean. During this journey, I gained a lot of weight and found myself weighing around 240 pounds. Can you believe it? Yes, I was once at 240 pounds. I eventually decided to lose the weight and hired a nutritionist to help me reach my goal of 190 pounds. I will not bore you with the details, but spoiler alert, I eventually hit my target. The most important part of that story, however, was something my nutritionist taught me that still sticks with me today: "One salad won't make you skinny, and one hamburger won't make you fat." It is about proportion and balance. That was when I realized the 80/20 rule applies not just to health but to all aspects of life, including leadership and personal growth.

Once I began following these principles and applying them in my personal life, I started to gain visibility and earn the trust of my audience. I had finally refined my skill set and built sustainable habits that made me more resilient to the ever-changing business environment, while also enabling me to reach a broader and more diverse group of peers. Over time, I was recognized as a credible subject matter expert in my field, respected by colleagues and industry professionals alike. Most importantly, I had established a strong set of core values that became the foundation of my growth and the compass for my continued journey.

Our core values are the principles that guide our decision-making and shape our leadership ability. Like a compass, they always point us in the right direction and form the foundation of our credibility. They align our actions with our brand, simply put, with what we stand for. Ultimately, core values strengthen both our influence and our thought leadership, and more importantly, they serve as the bridge of trust between us and our audience.

To the naked eye, this may seem straightforward, but after a few rounds of trial, error, and research, I quickly realized it was more complex than I had initially thought. Over time, I uncovered a hidden sequence I came to call the chain of trust, which forms the framework for how credibility grows. This became a memorable point in my journey, because it was the moment when the bigger picture finally came into view.

Before we delve into this in detail, let's first do some self-reflection to help us bring this framework to life.

Pause and Reflect Exercise

Take a few minutes to write down your honest answers to the following question.
- *What comes to mind when you think of your core values?*
- *How do they impact your decision-making?*
- *Do they reflect your personal brand?*

By answering these questions and reflecting on what you wrote, you will begin building the foundation needed to understand how your values, credibility, and trust are all interconnected.

Let's look more closely at this and start with the first link in the chain: Values. For your core values to be impactful, they must be clearly defined. If you cannot articulate them with clarity, they will remain abstract ideas rather than guiding principles. Clear values provide direction, inform decisions, and serve as the baseline for how others perceive your credibility.

So now, when you revisit your first answer from the "Pause and Reflect" Exercise, does the connection between values and credibility resonate with you? If it doesn't, that is okay. We are still building out the framework, and it will come into perspective soon enough, I promise. In the meantime, I want to share a personal anecdote to add a little color to our discussion.

When I first did this exercise, the usual hot topics immediately came to mind, such as trust, bravery, ethics, and integrity. Writing them down felt good, almost like checking a box. But after a moment of reflection, I realized I had no real understanding of what they meant to me in the context of core values, or how I was supposed to apply them directly to my life. That was when I realized I needed to dig deeper.

I had to put these deeply held beliefs and principles to work by researching their definitions, reflecting on why they mattered to me, and deciding how I wanted them to be reflected in my actions. This step was key, and it is something I encourage you to consider when defining or reevaluating your own unique set of core values. This matters because when your behaviors and actions are organically aligned, your core values are expressed authentically.

This alignment is the ultimate when you are building influence through thought leadership. You need alignment. When there is a misalignment, trust is destroyed and your audience will notice. Trust me, I have sat through plenty of presentations where words like "innovative" or "transparent" were peddled around, but when it came time to see the product, it was a different story. The innovation was underwhelming, and the so-called "transparent" pricing strategy left much to the end-user to discover in the small fine print. This experience left me confused, and in retrospect, was an excellent example of the impact alignment has on our leadership presence and overall influence.

A key factor in maintaining influence is not only building trust but also sustaining it. And how do you do that? By being consistent in your behavior. Trust is a state of psychological safety that emerges when people feel confident in the reliability and integrity of an individual. This is exactly the feeling we want to invoke in our audience when we write an article, lead a project, or step onto a stage for a speaking engagement.

It is a little tricky, though, because consistency is not achieved by simply making the proverbial statement, "I am innovative" or "I am transparent." Instead, it is built over time through our actions, words, and behaviors. You have probably heard the saying, "Don't just talk the talk; walk the walk." This is that moment. From here forward, I want you to live and breathe this principle as you continue your professional journey.

Trust is not given; it is earned in the real world. For me, this meant consistently delivering results and living up to my full potential. It went beyond academic qualifications, professional credentials, or impressive titles. It meant following through on what I said and being relentlessly dedicated to achieving outcomes by any means necessary.

When I reflected more deeply on this concept, I began paying closer attention to the words I chose and the way I showed up. For example, if I called myself "transparent," was I truly being open about my failures and missteps? Could my colleagues trust that I was honest and authentic during speaking engagements, or was I only highlighting my wins and polishing up the rough edges of my story for likes and applause?

This was another turning point in my journey, one that required a micro-adjustment to align my values, my words, and my actions, which ultimately allowed me to achieve the results I wanted. Figuring this out was pivotal because it helped me not only build trust but also project it consistently to my audience.

This is the crux of our discussion, and one of the most important lessons I hope you take away from this part of the journey: trust equals credibility, and credibility equals trust. The two work hand-in-hand, and you cannot have one without the other. Here is a little-known secret: as you build one, the influence of the other grows substantially, creating a powerful cycle that strengthens your leadership and amplifies your impact. Gaining influence, trust, and credibility is the ultimate reward for successfully navigating the earlier stages. This recognition not only elevates your standing, but also expands your ability to influence, attracts loyalty, and provides social proof for others who are observing your journey.

> *"Influence is not found in being the smartest, but in being the wisest."* — Dr. George J. McLean

This is where we put all the pieces of the puzzle together and begin defining our own unique value proposition. Before moving forward, we must pause to ask an essential question: *Why should someone choose to listen to you?* Defining your value proposition is about articulating the distinct perspective, expertise, and insights you bring to the table that set you apart from others in your field.

With this in mind, let's start with a brief review of my personal answer to that question. I wanted people to listen to what I had to say because I had built a long, meaningful academic and professional career, filled with learning lessons and insights that I believed held enormous value in the business world.

But to do this, we must take deliberate steps to frame our unique value proposition. Step one takes us back to a concept we explored in Chapter 2: focusing on what you are good at, rather than spreading yourself too thin. As humans, we are constantly tempted to try to be good at everything, but influence is built by narrowing your focus and becoming an expert in your chosen field.

Now that we have revisited this concept, it is time to put it into practice. Earlier, we identified what makes us experts. Now, we must take the next step and decide what we are genuinely good at—the skills and abilities that form the backbone of our unique value proposition. The truth is, we all believe we are good at certain things, but in reality, some of those areas may not be worth our time or energy. Part of this process is learning to recognize when we should shift our focus elsewhere, doubling down on the strengths that set us apart.

I narrowed my direct expertise into strategic advising, and guess what? I was good at it. I loved the thrill of researching new ideas and bringing a unique perspective to the table. Naturally, one of the questions I always get during these conversations at seminars is, "Dr. McLean, how do you know you're good at it?" And that is a very valid question. As I've said before, we all think we are good at something, but implicit bias combined with confirmation bias often distorts our reality. The answer, however, is straightforward, and you don't need a PhD to put it into action. Look outward and pay attention to the signals from your colleagues and peers. These often show up in the form of performance reviews, peer feedback, or even consistent compliments that point to your strengths.

Once we unpack what we are experts in, and what we are genuinely good enough at to share with others, the next step is deciding who we are going to share it with, and how. It may seem like the obvious next step, at least in my opinion, but it is surprisingly uncommon in practice. I have sat through plenty of industry conferences, and more times than not, I have walked away asking myself: *Why did they give this presentation here? Did they really think it was relevant to this audience?*

At the time, I honestly didn't think twice about it, but later in my career, it became one of those moments that highlighted just how important it is to choose your target audience when developing a robust value proposition. I learned this lesson the hard way. I was scheduled to speak at an industry conference in Kentucky, teaching a certification class that I assumed would be filled with junior leaders seeking credentials. I prepared an entire presentation, showed up early, and was ready to go.

Only one problem! When I walked to the podium and glanced at the attendee list, I realized the room was filled with directors and CEOs of their respective companies. I was extremely nervous and had to pivot quickly to make the presentation meaningful for senior leadership. Fortunately, my background in education gave me the tools to adapt. I transitioned from a lecture-style format to an open-forum discussion, which I knew would be effective for senior leaders to engage and learn.

That experience taught me a valuable lesson about the importance of knowing and studying my audience. Now, before any presentation, meeting, speaking engagement, or even when I publish a blog, the second question I always ask after choosing the topic is,

Who is the audience, and why should they care? I encourage you to take a moment here to pause and reflect.

Pause and Reflect Exercise

Take a few minutes to write down your honest answers to the following questions:

- Did you truly know your target audience the last time you gave a presentation, led a speaking event, or published a blog?
- If you did, was the topic and approach relevant to them?
- If not, what would you do differently in the future with this information?

Now that we have made it this far, and we've chosen our topic, identified our target audience, and clarified why they should care, it's time to narrow in on the specific problem we are addressing. I remember an old saying one of my professors used to tell me during my doctoral program: *"Go deep, not wide."*

At the time, my first thought was, *"What the hell does that even mean?"* But now, a few years wiser and a lot more seasoned, I can tell you exactly what it means: pick one problem and go all in. Examine it from every angle, test solutions, and "beat it to death" until you've uncovered insights that matter.

This is a major part of shaping your value proposition for your audience. Think about it, how many times have you sat through a class, presentation, or seminar, only to leave without a clear understanding of the solution? I know I've walked out of plenty of auditoriums more confused than when I walked in, which is a terrible outcome for both the speaker and the audience.

As we wrap up this framework, let's tackle the final two steps simultaneously, since, to me, they are essentially one and the same. Get it, my book? I know, lame joke. The final step is about showing differentiation and proving value. That meant developing a unique approach to solving a common problem. I had to focus on being different first, and innovative second. This was not as hard as it sounds, because, let's be honest, if the problem already had a clear solution, we wouldn't be here talking about it in the first place, right?

This was the key—learning the difference. Not every innovative approach is truly different, but if you start with being different, it naturally guides your path toward innovation. Whew! That's a mouthful. So, let me break it down.

I remember my first consulting job, where I was tasked with reviewing a pilot camera program in parking facilities, designed to reduce operational overhead. On the surface, this was not a unique idea; in fact, it was quite common. The real difference, however, was in the approach. The organization I worked with at the time was not profit-driven, which meant the challenge was not just about cutting costs, but also about finding a way to balance public perception with revenue generation.

What was too far? How do we balance the needs of the residents with the needs of the organization? At the end of the day, we were there to make money and provide a service to the community. That was it. The value wasn't in presenting an innovative idea. That wasn't what people wanted to hear about. They had already sat through countless presentations by sales agents, consultants, and industry leaders pitching the next big thing. The value came from my approach: what I had learned, what insights I could share that might save them time, and most importantly, what could save them money. Translating those findings into strategic insights was the hidden value.

"You can fake it until you make it, but once you make it, you can no longer fake it." — **Dr. George J. McLean**

It's now time to dig into your tactical toolbox for influence and figure out how to share these newly found insights in a way that adds value to your audience. This is the moment to "walk the walk" by bringing all the different pieces of the puzzle together to form what I call the "Bigger Picture." We've finally reached the stage of sharing this knowledge in the real world, outside of our heads. And this is where things truly get exciting.

So, let me ask you: what's the first thought that comes to mind when you imagine stepping onto a platform, or better yet, your personal soapbox? We're going to skip the Pause and Reflect Exercise here and get straight to the point.

When I first thought about it, the only image that came to mind was the big show, getting on stage, being the keynote speaker, sharing insights, and taking names. But soon after, I realized something important: it was much more than that. True influence meant leveraging multiple platforms, using social channels, writing articles and blogs, creating content calendars, and continuously studying and refining my message. It was bigger and more complex than I initially thought.

I had to learn the art of being my own brand ambassador. This meant not only promoting myself but also leveraging the right tools to enable others to promote me, amplifying my reach. That was my first real move into the big leagues. The starting point was becoming proficient with social media management tools—the tools of the trade, so to speak.

Here's the truth: we can accomplish incredible things in our communities and industries or even create unique content that adds substantial value to people's lives, but it is meaningless if we cannot effectively distribute it to the right audience. Visibility is the bridge between value and influence, and without it, your impact never leaves the room.

Social media management programs make this easier by allowing you to schedule posts, share your insights, and publish across multiple channels simultaneously. They empower you to use digital platforms as a strategic tool to amplify your voice.

But digital distribution is not the only way to get your message out to the world; it is simply the most accessible. One of the most consistent and impactful methods remains speaking engagements, where you connect with an audience directly and establish influence in real time. The challenge, however, is that the average person has no idea where to start.

I can relate to this firsthand. Over the years, I have spoken at events across the United States, hosting shop talks, teaching certification courses, and sitting on industry panels. Each of these opportunities was an incredible experience, but I will admit, getting my foot in the door was one of the hardest parts of the journey. It was more than establishing credibility and having a strong brand in the industry. I had to get myself in front of the right people, because speaking engagements are one of those funny things that are invite-only. Once you get your chance, it is sink or swim, plain and simple, because you are only as good as the last event.

I remember my first speaking event that was sanctioned by an international conference. I was hosting a panel that included my CEO at the time, and my role was to facilitate the conversation and keep the audience engaged. But before I get too far ahead, let me explain how I earned the opportunity to lead this event.

I took the long road, gradually gaining the attention of industry leaders by organizing educational events and serving on committees that selected speakers. It took more than three years of sweat and tears before I was finally given the chance to host. And even then, the opportunity only came because the original speaker had to cancel at the last minute after contracting COVID-19.

In that moment, I was thrilled to finally be on stage, but I was also curious. After the panel, I pulled one of the other speakers aside and asked if there was an easier way to secure future opportunities.

His answer was straightforward, and it changed everything for me. What he shared became the foundation of a mini framework for landing speaking engagements, and lucky for you, I am going to share it here to save you countless hours of trial and error.

Here is exactly what he taught me, the practical steps that turned opportunity into predictable results.

The first step is to create a dedicated speaker page that highlights your craft. This may sound sophisticated, but it does not have to be. I used LinkedIn. At the time, I was not popular enough to justify having a personal website, but I could use a platform where I had already built a following to showcase my portfolio. On my page, I included my bio, speaking topics, previous engagements, and testimonials.

At the time of writing this book, I still keep one platform updated and active. In fact, I recently used it to promote a panel at a local conference here in Miami. This simple step allowed me to position myself as a speaker, not just a professional who occasionally speaks. It created a clear, accessible point of reference for anyone considering me for future opportunities.

Then I had to document it. There is an adage that says, "If you didn't record it, it didn't happen." That was the mindset I applied here. Pictures and video clips live far longer than the moment itself, and they expand the reach of your message well beyond the room you are in. This became a game-changer because it gave me the material I needed to promote both past and future speaking engagements.

I used LinkedIn as my repository, storing sound bites, video clips, articles, and flyers for upcoming events. The platform is naturally oriented toward professional growth, which made it the perfect space to reach my target audience while also building credibility in the industry. The best part was that it allowed me to monitor my brand in real time and adjust along the way.

Applying this framework became the key to being booked for more speaking engagements. For the first time, I had a platform that allowed me to distribute my unique product, my insights, and perspective, directly to industry professionals.

I remember when I first started posting, I would get maybe four likes, at most. It was discouraging, to say the least. But here's the truth: don't let that stop you. You are your biggest advocate, and this is not Instagram. Just because you don't get a flood of likes or comments doesn't mean people aren't paying attention. LinkedIn is a professional environment, and many industry leaders observe quietly, moving in silence for their own reasons.

I learned this firsthand when I was invited to sit on a panel, and the organizer explained how they had been following my work from afar, and how my content was influencing the field. At first, I brushed it off, thinking they were just trying to close the deal. But the message hit home the second time I heard it during an later interview for an executive role. The City Manager told me he had heard my name multiple times, and that when he asked who the up-and-coming leaders were in the industry, my name came up repeatedly. That was the moment I saw the fruits of my labor. The consistency was paying off, and as I continued to follow these steps, I was booked for more and more opportunities.

This is where we tie it all together and paint the bigger picture. Up to this point, we have built the tools, frameworks, and habits needed to establish trust, credibility, and influence. Now the question becomes: how do we sustain it for the long term? Influence is not a one-time accomplishment; it is a continual journey of aligning your values, consistently showing up, and delivering authentic value to your audience.

Long-term influence requires discipline, intentionality, and a commitment to growth. It is about building a legacy that extends beyond individual achievements and creating an impact that resonates across industries, communities, and generations. In other words, it is no longer just about making a difference today; it is about positioning yourself as a trusted and credible voice for tomorrow.

We must make a commitment to long-term learning and evolution. To this day, professional development is the cornerstone of my growth. It is something I prioritize daily; I am always researching and finding new ways to improve my craft. This could mean refining my public speaking, staying current with industry trends, developing new materials, or serving on boards. Whatever the activity, it is always deliberate and focused on strengthening a specific quality. Remember, Rome was not built in a day. It took consistency and hard work. The same is true for leadership, and that is exactly what it will take to shape you into the leader I know you can become today.

The one that exudes trust and authenticity in their actions— that is who I ultimately became, and it is who I hope you grow into after reading this chapter. By making consistent, credible contributions, we begin creating perspectives that rise above popular opinion or fleeting trends, delivering true value and setting ourselves apart. That is the key. We must shift from short-term thinking and instant gratification to long-term focus and perseverance, where the reward is delayed but far more meaningful.

To close this chapter of our journey, I want to leave you with a few suggestions:

- Always work to expand your understanding of your field of expertise.
- Relentlessly pursue self-development at all costs, even if it is just 15–20 minutes a day devoted to your craft.
- Share consistently. Share at every opportunity, no matter how big or small the stage may be. You are your own biggest advocate, and no one will promote you the way you can. You control your brand.
- Grow your network and be patient. Your network is your audience. I built mine painstakingly by searching LinkedIn and adding people one by one; it was like a modern version of cold calling, only digital.

Once you do this, the easier part begins. Be patient. The magic will happen. In fact, 90 percent of the time, it is already happening; you just have not noticed it yet. Your presence is growing, your influence is building, and soon, your network will expand organically. That is when you step into your own light and become a star in your own right. Until then, stay patient, stay consistent, and most importantly, have fun with the process.

Chapter 5

The Innovation Imperative

"Innovation distinguishes between a leader and a follower."
– Steve Jobs

Having the platform is definitely important and fundamental to establishing yourself as a leader in the industry. But to stay relevant, as we discussed in Chapter 4, you must interject your unique perspectives into the conversation.

This is where we take it a step further and uncover the importance of becoming a strategic innovator. In today's business environment, we need to understand the true meaning of the saying, "innovate or die." The skill of innovation is no longer optional; it is a requirement for survival and growth.

Ideally, our innovative spirit is what drives us to become thought leaders in our industries. We are doing more than just sharing ideas; we are advocating for our perspectives in a world of competing values. We believe in the power of these ideas with conviction, and we want others to believe in them too. That is exactly how I approached every engagement where I had the opportunity to share my perspective. It was an attitude I developed over the years: if I don't believe in it, why should you?

One of the keys to becoming a thought leader in any industry is understanding that, at its core, thought leadership is about being a change agent. True thought leaders inspire transformation through communication. They bring forward fresh perspectives and a vision that challenges the status quo, sparking the need for new practices and new directions. By promoting innovative ideas while fostering trust and alignment, they make it easier for others to accept and participate in change. This is how thought leaders turn vision into reality and ensure their organizations continue to grow and adapt in an ever-changing landscape.

> *"Any fool can see what is directly in front of them, but only a true leader has the vision to see around corners."*
> — Dr. George J. McLean

To be a thought leader, you must be a visionary—someone who can see beyond what is directly in front of them, and anticipate what is coming, all while accounting for how the landscape continues to evolve. Thought leaders take foresight and transform it into actionable insights, often through trial and error, which ultimately underpins true innovation in the business environment. I call this the foundation of the executive mindset—a concept we will explore in greater detail in later chapters.

I first began to understand this lesson early in my career when I met the COO of the organization where I worked, who would later go on to become our CEO. We were discussing changing the fees at one of our facilities. At the time, I was hyper-focused on revenue generation and had not considered the political backlash we would receive from business owners and residents.

The COO at the time quickly showed me it was not just about the numbers, it was about anticipating these challenges and turning them into opportunities. Instead of avoiding political pressure, we could leverage it to gain favor, positioning the change as a strategic advantage. Even more, they emphasized the importance of innovative thinking: using technology to offset costs for residents while shifting more of the burden to visitors, who traditionally held no voting power in our districts.

It was a genius approach and a turning point for me. That moment revealed how much my thinking needed to evolve if I ever wanted to thrive in the executive ecosystem. I had to become comfortable operating outside my comfort zone by challenging the status quo of the industry. It was then I realized that leaders are not just facilitators of change; they are the catalysts that drive it forward.

Pause and Reflect Exercise

Take a few minutes to write down your honest answers to the following questions:
- *Has there been a moment when you only focused on what was directly in front of you?*
- *How would your thinking need to evolve to be considered executive level?*
- *How could you reframe your thinking with an innovative mindset to move your industry forward?*

When we question long-standing norms, whether industry-wide or within our organizations, we create the path for a new way of thinking. This is the road less traveled, but it often leads to innovation and growth.

I remember working at a large tech company (which I will not name here), whose core values included encouraging healthy conflict whenever someone presented a new idea. The premise was simple: this conflict often produced the best version of an idea, because no matter who you were, your colleagues were expected to play devil's advocate and challenge your way of thinking. It is important to note that they were not looking for "negative Nancys." Instead, they understood that to grow quickly, resilience in your thinking was essential.

The latent effect of this process was that pressure testing every idea, built trust and helped establish credibility. We knew no one was shooting from the hip and every idea was properly vetted, which strengthened the innovative impact it had on the industry. Looking back now, I realize this was not just a procedural task; it was shaping our thinking process to help us see the bigger picture. This was important, not only because it filtered out the noise in our ideas, but also because it ensured that our ideas aligned with the mission and vision of our organization.

As a leader today, I often hear great innovative ideas, but the first question I ask is, "Does this align with the goals of your organization?" In a world where technology is so prevalent, we are often enticed to try anything and everything in the pursuit of profits or market dominance. But this approach is misguided and does not fit the mold of the executive mindset we are building.

To be innovative leaders, it is not just about becoming comfortable operating in the abyss where others cannot see the outcome. It is about finding a problem and developing a solution that is not only innovative but also aligned with the bigger picture of the organization. And that bigger picture does not have to be limited to what the organization is today. It can also reflect where you envision it in the future.

As thought leaders, we must first become change agents and stay true to our purpose. It is the big "why." Why do we put forth the effort to master our craft? Why do we invest endless hours into professional development? Why do we take the time to share our insights and findings? Why do we even bother? We could easily keep these discoveries to ourselves, but we don't.

It is because we are part of a small cohort of people who understand that it is bigger than us. We are the change agents who shepherd transformation within our organizations. This was something new to me once, and it may be new to you now. But let me tell you that it is an amazing feeling, not only because our opinions are valued, but because our industry would not survive without people like us who push the limits every day. We have moved beyond practicing theories to creating them for others who will follow in our footsteps. All we need to do is find the white space and challenge the norms that are taken for granted. The essence of thought leadership is to create where others follow; to lead where others hesitate.

When we create, we create. There's something exciting about solving the unique problems that plague our industry. But let's pause here and dial in on what we really mean by "creation" in this space, because it's easy to get confused. I know I was at first.

For full disclosure, we are not in the business of creating problems; we are here to solve them. That is where the importance of identifying the white space comes into play. White space is where opportunity lives. It's the gap between what exists today and what could exist tomorrow, and it's our job as innovators to see it, define it, and build solutions that bring it to life.

Now, if this concept is new to you, or if you are a junior leader just starting out, I can imagine you have a few burning questions: "*How do I find a problem?*" Or even better, "*How do I find a problem to solve that is important enough for people to care about?*"

The answer lies in uncovering the unmet needs of your industry. These are the issues your peers, colleagues, media, or anyone invested in your field genuinely care about solving. Before I learned about white space, I often made the mistake of coming up with a solution first and then searching for a problem to attach it to. Let's just say that approach was less than successful, and more often than not, it led me straight into a brick wall.

But discovering white space was game-changing for my career. To make this concept more digestible, I developed a mini framework from my own experiences. My hope is that you can use these same strategies to identify and leverage white space in your own journey.

For starters, I became a student of my customers. They are the heart and soul of our companies and ultimately, what keeps the lights on at night. I listened to them closely to better understand problems that our current services or products did not address. I paid attention to customer feedback, conducted market research, and reached out to observe common frustrations.

The second leg is a little more nuanced, and you must be careful because there is often a lot of noise in customer data. I reviewed my customer base and studied which products and services they used most frequently, and from there, I identified a niche in the industry.

For me, this turned out to be customers who only utilized our facilities during vacation. Interestingly, the problem was that our existing rate structure was not flexible enough to accommodate them, and we needed a quick and easy solution. We solved this by developing a new product specifically designed to serve that customer group, which allowed us to capture additional revenue while meeting the needs of our community.

Now, this may sound like an oversimplification, but it demonstrates the real-world power of applying this strategy effectively.

The next step is studying emerging trends. This is something we should all do as professionals, but it is worth calling out because many of us do not make it a regular practice. As leaders, we must pay attention to shifts in technology, consumer behavior, and social values. The insights we gather help us anticipate how these trends will reshape the industry. This allows us to stay ahead of the curve and prepare for upcoming challenges before they arrive.

Lastly, and probably the most practical step of the framework, is analyzing competitors. All this really means is studying your competitors to identify either a competitive advantage they hold or a shortfall they are failing to address. Once identified, you can strategically step in to fill the gap by developing an innovative solution of your own.

Once we have clearly defined the problem, the next step is to develop a solution. As we stated earlier, this is done by challenging the status quo and industry norms. But how do we do this? It begins with asking the most powerful question of all: Why? We must always position ourselves as truth seekers. Instead of simply accepting existing processes and long-held beliefs, we need to ask probing, thoughtful questions that uncover the root causes of issues.

But it cannot stop at rejecting the norm: we must also offer alternatives that reshape the current narrative. This is where we step into the role of visionaries. Visionaries set the tone by presenting new perspectives backed by research, data, and actionable insights. They use these tools to spark dialogue, take risks, and pursue solutions on a larger scale. By doing so, they provoke new thinking and inspire others to move the industry forward.

The innovative ideas we develop must align with the mission and vision of the organization to push it forward. But what does this really mean? Let's briefly explore this concept in greater depth, because it has some of the strongest implications for both individual and organizational success.

The innovative insights you shape need to be tied to the core purpose of the company you represent, or if you're independent, to your own personal mission and vision. Without this alignment, ideas risk becoming random thoughts that, for lack of a better word, feel like shooting from the hip. That kind of approach dilutes your value as a thought leader and leaves your audience questioning your direction.

Alignment provides clarity and a shared sense of purpose. Imagine attending a technology conference , only to have a panelist start talking about innovative solutions for closing the achievement gap in secondary education. No matter how valuable the idea might be, you would probably feel confused. It would be a classic wrong place, wrong time moment. This example highlights why anchoring your ideas to the mission at hand is so important, as it ensures relevance, resonance, and impact.

To accomplish this, we must first develop a deep understanding of our organization's mission and vision statement. For those of us who work within a company, this means learning it, internalizing it, and using it as the guiding star for our ideas and innovations.

For entrepreneurs, guess what? You must define your own mission and vision statement. Yes, you heard that right. The reason I stress this is because, often, when I ask entrepreneurs about their mission or vision, they either give me something vague and unclear, or admit they don't have one at all. Without that clarity, your ideas and innovations won't have the focus or direction needed to build credibility and lasting influence.

So, first things first. Let's work to clearly define and refine these mission and vision statements, whether they belong to your organization or whether they're your unique statements. The best way to do this is by breaking the statements into smaller parts and placing them into buckets that can each be tied to a verb.

Take this example:

"My mission is to help professionals unlock consistent habits of leadership through practical frameworks and reflective learning."

Here's how it breaks down:

- **Who are you serving?**

    "Professionals"

    A mission must identify a clear audience—the people who benefit from your work. In this case, it's working adults, leaders, or aspiring leaders.

- **What are you helping them do?**

    "Unlock consistent habits of leadership."

    This defines the transformation. It's not just about leadership in general; it's specifically about building habits that stick.

- **How are you doing it?**

    "Through practical frameworks and reflective learning"

    Every mission statement should explain the method or approach—the way you plan to deliver the transformation.

By completing this process, you will be able to unlock the true meaning of your mission and vision statement. This clarity puts you in a stronger position to integrate new ideas into the framework you have already developed. It ensures that your innovations do not occur in a vacuum, but instead, fit into the bigger picture, remaining focused, relevant, and impactful.

But we also have additional tools that can help us navigate the often complicated process of alignment. I know this is one of those things that is easier said than done. So, let's explore a tool that has been valuable in my journey—one that I hope will be just as beneficial for you: strategic planning. It is often talked about, but rarely done with true intent. I am here to tell you to use it. Simply put, strategic planning is one of the most powerful tools you have, whether at the organizational level or as an entrepreneur. It ensures not only alignment but, more importantly, measurable progress.

Strategic planning helps you articulate the future of your organization. This is where we take the notes we jotted down earlier about our mission and vision statements, and actually put them to work. We use this information to set strategic goals that bring these ideals to life. For example, if your mission is to "help others unlock consistent habits of leadership," the next step is to ask: What specific goals can we set to make this a reality, and how can we measure progress through either quantitative or qualitative data?

Now, you may be wondering how this ties back to thought leadership. Here's the answer: strategic planning is where innovative ideas stop being random sparks and instead become fuel for long-term impact. It ensures your creativity stays tethered to mission and vision, giving every idea both direction and purpose. This is how thought leaders transform innovation into influence— not by creating for creation's sake, but by aligning every action with the bigger picture and pushing it forward. That is the true innovation imperative.

At its core, strategic planning is the compass that guides us when making hard decisions about which problems deserve our organization's resources. Using our earlier mission example, this could mean evaluating the human capital of the workforce and identifying a need to upskill employees to meet the evolving demands of the business. The key is to ensure that every solution developed remains fully aligned with the mission and vision. At the end of the day, we are all innovators in our own right. What sets thought leaders apart is that we step to the forefront, we advocate, we share how we solved the problem, and we make the case for why others should care.

We create a shared purpose that drives others toward common objectives. This is one of the core reasons we share our ideas and advocate so strongly every single day. As we've said before, when we believe in something, we want others to take that same path, guided by the lessons we've learned and the conviction we carry. Once we have aligned these practices, we must commit to refining them daily. This means regularly assessing how innovations contribute to the mission and vision, and adjusting as needed.

However, it is important for me to warn you that while practicing alignment is essential, we must be careful not to stifle creativity in the process. As a leader, you will constantly face adversity, and that adversity often becomes the underlying force for creativity and growth. To navigate these challenges, it is vital to shift your focus toward innovative problem-solving. Approach obstacles with fresh perspectives rather than being confined by their limitations.

For instance, one of the biggest challenges that I guarantee you will face at one point in your career is budget and financial constraints. But I challenge you to reframe them through your innovative framework.

This can easily be done by following a few key steps. The first involves a bit of reverse engineering to arrive at a solution. What do I mean by that, and how does this apply to constraints? Before we get there, let's take a moment to define and emphasize the importance of limitations by clearly articulating their *perceived* boundaries. I use the word "perceived" intentionally, because most boundaries are not set in stone. Financial constraints are usually harder to navigate, but many others can be reimagined, stretched, or even overcome with the right mindset and strategy.

For example, if you are working with a small budget, study projects with larger budgets to spark ideas and uncover unconventional approaches for achieving your goals. Do not just accept the status quo.

This mentality has served me well many of times, over the course of my career. At a previous employer, I remember working as a junior leader on designing an experience for Customer Service Appreciation Week I was given a budget of $10,000 to purchase supplies, staff the event, and create social content. This was great. The only problem was that the videographer cost over 50 percent of the entire budget.

At first, I was discouraged, but instead of giving up, I challenged the status quo and researched other events online. I noticed that multiple events seemed to be filmed on an iPhone. This was something I had not considered, but it was easily accessible and would reduce the budget by 25 percent if I only had to outsource the editing of the video.

I will not get into the weeds here, but let's just say this simple trick turned the project around in time to be completed.

You can also force new perspectives by setting your own constraints or audacious goals for your projects. I've said it before, and I'll say it again: the best outcomes are born from conflict and debate. When you place unreasonable constraints on yourself, it forces you to think strategically and develop a solution from a new perspective.

Here are some simple things that worked for me and, hopefully, will work for you. By the way, when you get good at them, I can say they are quite a fun exercise to complete. Firstly, force connections between two unrelated concepts to see what will emerge from the exercise. For example, parking and cell phones. These seem completely unrelated at first thought, but then, suddenly, I think of applications, GPS, notifications, and my creativity comes to life with all these great ideas.

This simple exercise shows us that innovation often comes from unlikely connections. By training your brain to look beyond the obvious, you unlock a creative edge that others may overlook.

Another tool is *timeboxing*. This one is straightforward. Set an unreasonable time limit for yourself and just brainstorm. Force your mind into decisive, rapid thinking, and jot everything down without judgment. Have fun with it. Sometimes, overthinking is our worst enemy, and the best way to cut through the noise is to get the ideas out of your head and onto paper.

A strategy that goes hand-in-hand with this is working with *limited resources.* Give yourself a small or unusual set of tools and let the magic happen. When you put yourself in uncomfortable situations, you tend to be at your most creative and innovative.

For an extra challenge, try combining the two: set a time limit and restrict your resources at the same time. You'll be surprised how much you can unlock under pressure.

While we wrap up this point, I want you to remember that this is an iterative process. It will often generate multiple ideas that will sometimes compete with one another in priority. Do not worry and do not raise the red flag. This is where I want to show you the power of the word "and." You can reduce wait times and simultaneously improve customer satisfaction. You can create a new application and connect it to a parking garage guidance system to find a location. It is never an either-or situation.

Start with the current state and your goal. Then, remove one key element, for example, a product's power cord, and brainstorm possible substitutes, like a battery. This simple shift forces you to explore new options and often reveals innovative paths you might not have considered before. The more you practice this, the more natural it becomes, and soon, you'll train yourself to see opportunities where others only see limits.

Practicing this will help you use innovation as a tool to future-proof your influence through thought leadership. By strategically combining foresight, continuous learning, and authentic communication, you build long-term credibility and relevance, creating a lasting impact rather than just temporary visibility. This is the key to it all and cornerstone of the thought leadership. We need to consistently deliver unique, valuable, and forward-thinking ideas that challenge the status quo.

And do not forget to leverage technology. It is your ally, and in the world of ChatGPT (yes, you heard that right!), you have a tool on your side that can offer tremendous value. This tool gives you the power to generate predictive insights, identify gaps, and forecast challenges. With this information, you are empowered to make strategic, data-driven decisions.

This is where you begin developing the ability to see around corners and move beyond the limitations of what is directly in front of you. You will start anticipating future scenarios, building contingency plans, and shifting from playing defense to offense. The game will no longer be checkers; it will be chess, and you will be prepared for the long haul.

Innovation becomes a mindset rather than a single event. You begin to crave the challenge of solving the complex problems that others in the industry avoid. This is what makes you a true change agent who not only understands but also embodies the innovative imperative. And that is the lesson of this chapter—innovation is not a tool you pick up once; it is a way of thinking that defines your leadership. It is the difference between being a follower and becoming a leader who shapes the future.

Chapter 6

Navigating Disruption with Confidence

"In the middle of difficulty lies opportunity." – Albert Einstein

Having the ability to navigate disruption with confidence is where you begin to harness the true power of leadership. Up to this point, we have explored tools and strategies that help you move beyond simply leading, toward becoming a change agent and a recognized thought leader in your field. You have made it this far, and my hope is that you have gained both insight and confidence from the lessons shared. From this point forward, we will begin to regard you as a thought leader in your own right, and transitioning into strategies for leading with vision, influence, and purpose.

Disruption is often used today as a characteristic of an organization. We hear it all the time: "we are disruptors of this or that industry." It has become a common phrase, but do we really understand what disruption means in the business environment? Disruption is a significant and sudden shift to an established order, system, or market. It is not the same as innovation. Innovation focuses on improving an existing system or process, while disruption fundamentally alters or replaces it altogether.

Disruption takes different shapes and forms, depending on the context in which it is applied. Some of the most common areas where disruption occurs include technology, society, and the economy. Before we go too far, it is important to note that while we may discuss these independently, they do not exist in isolation. Each one often influences and amplifies the others, creating ripple effects that redefine industries and leadership strategies.

Let me show you what I mean, as we begin the next leg of our journey. We will start with the most well-known form of disruption: technological disruption. This refers to innovations that fundamentally change how industries, businesses, and people operate. There are countless examples, but I want to share one that is close to my heart, because, earlier in my career, I worked for a major ride-sharing technology company and experienced this transformation firsthand

I remember that as a kid (I will probably give away my age to the younger audience here), our only options for transportation outside of owning a car were taxis and the bus. When we needed a ride, we often had to borrow a car or rely on a friend. In sunny South Florida, taxis were expensive, and the bus was not always practical, especially in the heat. Then ride-sharing came along and completely disrupted the taxi market by making rides more affordable and accessible.

It was brilliant. Instead of calling a traditional taxi company, I could now open an application on my phone and request a ride with just a few taps. The convenience was unmatched, and the impact on the industry was undeniable. At the time, this was not commonly referred to as disruption, but it was the very shift that put ride-sharing companies on the map among business scholars and professionals as a prime example of a disruptive innovator.

Then we have social disruption, which is less commonly mentioned, but equally important to understand. Why is this significant? Because it involves sudden and profound changes to the normal functioning of society and its communities. And we all have a powerful and relevant example, regardless of age: COVID-19. The pandemic forced schools to close, required businesses to implement six-foot social distancing rules, and brought community activities to a halt. This was a truly historic moment that disrupted the way society functions and reshaped it forever. It is not the only example of social disruption, but it is one of the most prominent, and is one that nearly everyone can relate to, in some way, because it touched all our lives in unique and personal ways.

And last, but not least, we have economic disruptors. This type of disruption is a little different from the others because its impact often depends on social class. One of the most common examples we are experiencing at the time of writing this book is the emergence of artificial intelligence. AI has had a profound effect on the business environment, displacing certain jobs while simultaneously creating entirely new ones. This shift has created an imbalance in the workforce, as AI continues to automate tasks once performed by humans. The most significant impact has been on entry-level positions, traditionally held by members of the lower class, such as clerical and administrative work, telemarketing, data entry, and various customer service roles.

This ongoing shift in the workforce is disrupting the way businesses think about talent, operations, and finances. Taken together, technological, social, and economic disruptions are converging in today's business environment, creating both a profound challenge and a unique opportunity for the modern leader. This is where a leader must step into their role as a change agent, navigating the chaos and putting every tool we have discussed into practice. In times of crisis, it is our responsibility to provide stability and direction, by showing empathy, making decisive choices, and offering unique insights that inspire others to move forward with confidence.

This is an important point to make. As leaders, we are expected to be the anchor that maintains composure, so our teams do not panic. And here is a little-known secret: the higher you rise in an organization, the more people will look to you in times of crisis for guidance and stability. So how do you weather the storm? Let me share a few lessons I have learned over the past fifteen years in both my academic and professional careers.

True leaders demonstrate emotional resilience by setting the emotional tone for their teams. They can process stress, adapt to challenges, and bounce back from setbacks, all while maintaining a positive outlook that inspires confidence in others. In my opinion, this is the most important factor in navigating chaos in the twenty-first century. But let's keep going, so you can be the judge for yourself.

The next point is making the well-being of others a priority. Sometimes, as leaders, we project confidence to reassure our teams, but in doing so, we risk crossing the line into arrogance. When that happens, it can create emotional conflict for junior team members. We need to show empathy by acknowledging that a situation is difficult and by allowing ourselves to be human. We are not robots, and we do not need to act like emotionless machines to exude confidence.

This truth became very clear to me in the latter part of my career. I was managing a large team at a tech company when we faced our first major crisis management situation. We were charged with launching a large-scale leasing operation for a tech company but ran into serious challenges qualifying leaseholders for insurance so they could drive the vehicles. Eventually, we found a way to help them get insured regardless of their financial situation. However, we were soon hit with a lawsuit and a cease and desist order from a competitor.

Now, on the surface, this may not have seemed like a full-blown crisis. It could easily have been dismissed as the cost of doing business. But internally, the impact was massive. The lawsuit rattled every employee. It sparked fear, created hysteria, and quickly grew into a media nightmare that made it appear as if we were doing something wrong. Morale collapsed. People stopped coming to work; people stopped believing. That was the real crisis.

At that moment, I had two choices. I could project extreme confidence that bordered on arrogance, or I could show empathy, acknowledge the difficulty of the situation, and lead with confidence by being solution-oriented. I chose empathy. Instead of pretending that everything was fine, I gathered my team together and spoke directly to the fear and uncertainty they were experiencing.

The lesson I learned was simple, but profound. In times of disruption or crisis, people do not want a leader who only looks confident. They want a leader who is real, who understands their fears, and who has the courage to address those fears while still pointing the way forward. That combination of empathy and direction is what transforms chaos into resilience and panic into progress.

As you can see, this is all grounded in communication. I call it strategic communication, which brings us to our next point. Effective communication is one of the strongest tools we have to combat uncertainty and misinformation. If we cannot communicate clearly and consistently as leaders, our teams, colleagues, and peers will never follow us or feel the psychological safety required to navigate a crisis.

This is not complicated. We must learn to conceptualize the situation and communicate it effectively. As much as you may think you are not required to share information with your subordinates, let me tell you now that you are wrong. Information is key, and transparency is golden. Your team needs to understand what is happening, within reason, and how it will impact them directly.

This step is critical for maintaining morale in the company. Best practice is to be transparent about the information that is known, to share it when it becomes known, and to be honest about what remains unknown. Doing so will not only prevent unnecessary panic, but will also help build, and, in many cases, strengthen trust.

Following these steps allows leaders to take decisive and adaptive action. When a crisis arises, a leader must act in the moment and remain adaptable to a changing environment. In those critical moments, it is not enough to talk about solutions; it is about taking action. Leaders must move beyond conversations and serve their teams with clarity and commitment. In times of crisis, leadership is rooted in servant leadership, where the focus shifts from authority to support, and from control to service.

Leaders can pivot in times of need, adjusting their strategies to respond to a constantly evolving landscape. We must remain flexible in our approach and understand that there is no "one size fits all" policy to solve the world's problems. To be effective problem solvers, we must stay dynamic and nimble in our decision-making.

When we become rigid in our approach, unintended consequences follow, such as stifled innovation, slower progress, and diminished creativity. This happens when we fall into the trap of the big mistakes. We stop listening, we stop learning, and ultimately, we stop leading. We become tyrannical in our behavior, closed off to new perspectives, and resistant to change.

Leadership requires balance, conviction paired with flexibility and openness. Effective leaders have the courage to adapt, to pivot when circumstances demand it, and to view change not as a threat but as an invitation to evolve. It is important that we, as leaders, use this understanding as the foundation of our framework for decision-making under pressure.

We all need the ability to be decisive, but no one more so than a leader. A lack of decisiveness can quickly undermine credibility in the eyes of your team, colleagues, and peers. In times of crisis, people will look to you for answers and reassurance, seeking stability and psychological safety when uncertainty looms.

This is no easy task, but there are frameworks that can help guide you along the way. I am going to share my top four. As we know, there is no single approach that fits every situation, so we must develop a repertoire of tools at our disposal for effective decision-making. The first one is my personal favorite, because it applies to a wide range of circumstances and provides a clear path for navigating complexity with confidence.

It is called the OODA Loop, and it was originally developed as a military strategy. The reason it is so powerful is that it has been tried and tested to support decision-making in fast-paced, constantly evolving situations. It breaks decision-making into a few simple steps that, once you connect all the dots, will present a full picture of the situation.

In the grand scheme of things, the OODA Loop is simple and straightforward. The first step is to observe. As a leader, you need information to make an informed decision. Rather than reacting impulsively with limited knowledge, take the time to gather and assess all available information before deciding on a course of action.

Now, I want to be frank. There will be times when you will not have access to all the information you need, or when time simply does not allow for a thorough analysis. In those moments, you must rely on what we discussed earlier—Act. Leadership requires the ability to make confident, timely decisions, even when the data is incomplete.

The next step is to orient yourself. Take a step back and analyze the situation from an outside perspective, identifying potential threats and risks. Sometimes, we are quick to make decisions, but fail to consider their broader impact. Every decision has ripple effects and unintended consequences that can reach far beyond our immediate circle.

For example, if you decide to lay off 25 percent of your workforce to save the company, the impact is often felt, not only by other departments and teams, but also by the customers they serve. Understanding these secondary and tertiary effects helps leaders make more balanced, ethical, and sustainable decisions.

Then you move to the next step—decide. This is where you determine the best course of action and put your plans into motion. You have gathered the information, analyzed it, and now, it is time to turn those insights into action. Taking these steps allows you to make informed decisions swiftly and confidently. The best part is that by following this process, you are better prepared to adapt and pivot, as new and relevant information becomes available along the way.

The next strategy is the 10-10-10 Rule, created by author Suzy Welch. It is an extremely valuable tool used to evaluate the long-term impact of our decisions. This framework is simple yet powerful, because it helps us separate emotion from logic to avoid lasting consequences.

When we make decisions in real time with limited information, emotions can easily influence our judgment. As leaders, we must learn to separate emotion from the decision-making process. This can be challenging, especially when we are passionate about our work, but trust me when I say this: a decision made purely out of emotion is rarely disciplined or sound. On a larger scale, emotionally driven decisions can have serious consequences at the enterprise level.

This is where the 10-10-10 Rule comes into play. By asking ourselves three simple questions: How will I feel about this decision in 10 minutes? ... 10 months? ... 10 years? We can filter out emotional impulses and make more grounded choices. It may not be a foolproof system, but it is a quick and effective way to stay nimble and fast while maintaining discipline and clarity in your leadership.

But we are not quite done yet. Let's look at a decision-making model framed by none other than Jeff Bezos, called the one-way versus two-way door framework. When I first learned about this model, I was genuinely curious about both the name and the value behind it.

As leaders, our time is extremely valuable. Each of these frameworks has its own merit, but one of the most common questions I get from my business students is, "Do we really have time to apply all of these models in the real world?" Before we look at this from a time standpoint, let's first review the concept itself.

The one-way versus two-way door model distinguishes between reversible and irreversible decisions.

One-Way Door: High-stakes, permanent decisions that require slow, thoughtful deliberation.

Two-Way Door: Reversible decisions that can be made quickly because you can always adjust or change course.

Bezos suggests that we use this process to guide our decision-making approach. To do this, we must examine the characteristics of a decision and determine its potential implications for the organization. However, the challenge is that some decisions have latent effects—impacts that are not immediately visible, but can surface years or even decades later, sometimes carrying significant long-term consequences for the company.

This is an important point to consider. I remember working on an amendment to a 99-year contract written for a mixed-use development that did not account for changes in technology and consumer behavior. Decades later, this oversight created unforeseen challenges for facility management. When the original contract was drafted, advancements in technology were not considered, and making any modifications became incredibly complex, because approval was required from the building's board of directors.

It is not to say that the original decision was poor. In fact, the contract was extremely well-written for its time. But as the COVID 19 pandemic accelerated technological innovation by nearly 10 to 15 years, the contract's limitations became clear. These were consequences no one could have reasonably predicted.

And that is where the real challenge lies: understanding that even well-informed, strategic decisions can have ripple effects far into the future. As leaders, we must use these tools thoughtfully, always considering both the immediate and long-term implications of our choices.

Lastly, we have the 4R test, which is another tool that can be used to evaluate the broader implications of your decision for all stakeholders. This test is more personal in nature, and one that leaders should use to evaluate how the decision will impact them personally. I like this one and use it on a regular basis with both my personal and professional decisions. It helps me understand the full implications of my decision. It allows for one to look at a decision from a strategic place and from different angles.

Regret: How much will you regret failing to act?

Repeal: How difficult would it be to reverse your decision?

Repercussions: What is the full scope of your decision's impact?

Resilience: How will your decision affect your personal resilience and that of others?

This framework helps us think beyond the immediate outcome and reflect on the emotional, practical, and ethical implications of our decisions. It serves as a reminder that every choice we make carries weight and affects not only our organizations, but also our own growth as leaders.

Now, to circle back and finally address that lingering question about our time... In a world of competing priorities, do we really have time to put these frameworks to use in the real world? The answer is yes. The goal of a framework is to guide your decision-making by giving you a set of tools. If you have the time to sit down for a brainstorming session, write out each point, and conduct a thorough analysis. That's great! But I would imagine that most of the time, we do not.

We operate in a world where every second counts, and if we fail to act in the moment, we risk missing opportunities. However, that does not mean we cannot be strategic, disciplined, and thoughtful in our decision-making as leaders. What we need is balance. These strategies are flexible and can be adapted to fit your unique situation and leadership style.

I do my best thinking in the shower, when I finally have a moment to reflect and digest. I often use the notes app on my phone to quickly evaluate decisions and jot down key considerations. When I do not have time to do that, I take five minutes to step away and collect my thoughts, or I call a trusted friend to talk through the problem and possible solutions. These are all ways I apply these strategies in the real world, both formally and informally, to guide my decision-making.

Once you begin making sound decisions, you will be able to communicate with stability and confidence. As you can see by now, confidence is a constant theme throughout our discussion of leadership. By this point, the word should personify you and your actions. It should be visible in how you speak, decide, and carry yourself.

If it already does, I guarantee people are noticing. And if it doesn't yet, don't worry; we'll continue to strengthen this trait in the chapters ahead. Confidence isn't built overnight. It's developed through repetition, reflection, and resilience. The more you apply it, the more it becomes second nature.

It is becoming increasingly important, now that we are strengthening our decision-making capacity and expanding the repertoire of tools at our disposal, to focus on how we communicate those decisions. We can be the world's best decision makers, but we must also be able to communicate our decisions confidently to groups of all sizes, with the same conviction and energy required to inspire action.

It is more than just projecting confidence. That is the necessary part we all perform in our everyday interactions. But true leadership requires that we not only appear confident, but that we genuinely believe in ourselves and our decisions. Ever heard the saying that a dog can smell fear? The same principle applies to confidence. Your team, colleagues, and peers can sense when you do not fully believe in yourself, and that lack of belief will weaken the impact of your message.

You must believe in your own credibility and root out every remnant of imposter syndrome that may still linger. It is common to experience imposter syndrome, especially when you are highly successful. We have all felt it at one point or another. No one is immune, including me. But if we can recognize this feeling, face it head-on, and overcome it, we will become far more powerful in our ability to execute with confidence and purpose.

This happened to me when I first became Dr. George McLean, after completing my Doctorate in Business Administration. I was one of those students who went straight through from high school to earning my doctorate, about fifteen years of being a student. During that same time, I worked and built a solid career as a mid-level manager, yet I never imagined the feeling I would have after finally becoming a subject matter expert in my field. It felt empty.

I was academically qualified but found myself reluctant to speak up in meetings or share my opinions. It was not a lack of experience that caused the hesitation; it was the fear of being wrong or being seen as a fraud. But was I really a fraud? Was I unprepared? These are the personal questions that many of us must confront and answer honestly if we want to break through this syndrome and lead with true confidence.

First, I had to understand the cause of what was happening to me before I could figure out how to move past it. Like everything in life, I discovered that imposter syndrome has many different causes, and it took a great deal of personal reflection to uncover the root of mine. We are going to talk about a few of the more common ones to see if they resonate with you as they did with me when I first discovered them.

The first thing I discovered was the underlying influence that your personality can have on how imposter syndrome manifests, especially during moments of great achievement. Have you ever received a compliment, award, or some other type of recognition, and instead of feeling happy, you ask yourself if you really deserve it? Instead of celebrating, you deflect the credit to someone else. Instead of smiling, you look away and avoid eye contact. That was me. And yes, that is a classic sign of personality-induced imposter syndrome.

What about your familial bonds and upbringing? Do you come from a family of high achievers where it seems like nothing is ever good enough or there is always more to accomplish? Sometimes, our parents think they are pushing us from great to excellent, but this can come with unintended consequences. It can negatively impact us as adults, making it difficult to accept compliments or feel proud of our achievements.

Then there is the pressure of high-stakes environments that can cause these feelings to resurface. Believe it or not, a high-pressure workplace can trigger imposter syndrome later in life. I have worked in a few places where feedback was not valued (it was frowned upon), and my manager gave the impression that their years of experience outweighed my education and expertise. I was made to feel like I was always wrong or late to the table with ideas. Despite my qualifications, I started to feel like I was not good enough to contribute meaningfully to the organization's mission. The social pressures of these types of environments only add to that dynamic.

When I finally took the time to reflect on these experiences, I realized that imposter syndrome is not about a lack of ability or achievement. It is about perception. It is rooted in the way we internalize pressure, expectations, and self-doubt. Whether it stems from our personalities, family influences, or work environments, the feeling is the same. We start questioning our worth, even when the evidence of our success is right in front of us. Recognizing this was a turning point for me. Once I could identify the root causes, I began to reclaim my confidence and remind myself that I had earned my place at the table.

So, how did I overcome it? I simply turned words into action, by taking a strategic approach and confronting imposter syndrome head-on. The first thing I did was reprogram the way I was thinking. I had to challenge the negative self-talk that was constantly running through my head. I took a step back and looked at myself from the outside, acknowledging my own skills and abilities.

Notice that I said *acknowledge*, not *compare*. This distinction is important. Comparison is the thief of joy, and I would never recommend using someone else as your benchmark. Focus on yourself, your qualifications, and your accomplishments. That is where your confidence and growth will come from.

We also need to track our progress daily, monthly, and yearly. Remember the adage we discussed? If you didn't write it down, it didn't happen? We must document our progress regularly and celebrate our achievements. We are qualified, and we do a lot, but we often overlook the smaller wins that add up over time.

This was my story. I served on advisory boards, volunteered with community organizations, and wrote numerous articles, yet I never took the time to write these accomplishments down. We must make it a habit to record them. Doing so allows us to measure our growth, year after year, and gives us the data we need to support the truth that we are qualified in everyone's eyes, including ours.

Then we have to talk about our concerns and say them out loud to a trusted friend or colleague. We need to have these difficult conversations and get feedback from others about our accomplishments and the areas where we still need to grow. We must know where we are starting to understand where we are heading. Once we put these thoughts into the atmosphere, we can begin to embrace our imperfections. We must understand that mistakes are a normal and essential part of learning and growth, not a personal failing.

Then we come to the final point. We must be aware of what is triggering these feelings. The reason I saved this point for last is because I wanted to first equip you with the tools to address the problem before emphasizing the importance of recognizing the trigger itself. When we are aware of the cause, we can take proactive steps to put our plan into action and address the root issue in real time.

For me, this trigger showed up in group settings at work, where I often felt intimidated by colleagues who had been working together for years and were extremely outspoken and assertive. I came in feeling timid and constantly questioned whether their years of experience outweighed my education. But once I identified this as a trigger, I began reviewing my accomplishments and accolades before big meetings and having conversations with a close friend to remind myself that I was fully capable. By doing this, I was able to tackle imposter syndrome head-on and prevent it from taking hold of me. Overcoming imposter syndrome doesn't happen overnight, but awareness, consistency, and self-belief will help you reclaim your confidence and lead with authenticity.

"Insecurity is loud, Confidence is Silent" — **Steve Magness**

Why did we start with external confidence before internal confidence? Because it is often easier to project confidence than to truly internalize it. I wanted to explore the background of this concept first to show that genuine, lasting confidence begins on the inside. External confidence can open doors, but internal confidence is what allows you to walk through them with purpose and authenticity.

External confidence is what you project to the world, and is largely performance-based, while internal confidence is rooted in your personal beliefs. It is the foundational trust in your own abilities, values, and judgment, which in turn fuels authentic thought leadership. Internal confidence is built on self-trust—the quiet conviction that you are capable, prepared, and worthy of the responsibilities you carry. This is why it is one of the most important traits we possess as leaders.

To clear up any confusion, it is essential to project confidence, even if you have not fully internalized it yet, but it is even more important to eventually develop and sustain that genuine internal belief. But what are the elements of this thing we call internal confidence? Is it just walking around like you are Harvey Specter from Suits? The king? The don? Some may say yes, but guess what? I am here to tell you, no. It entails far more than that, and we are going to discuss those elements now, so I can drive this point home.

If you want to be a self-aware leader, the first step is getting to know yourself on a deeper level. Confidence is more than thinking you are good; it is knowing that you are good. You achieve this by reflecting on your strengths, weaknesses, values, and personality. This is what I call the proverbial benchmark. It is a tool you can use to better understand yourself from an outside perspective and see who you really are. It allows you to identify that unique magic sauce that gives you the ability to successfully overcome adversity. This is the foundation of your confidence.

You also need to honestly accept the fact that you are not perfect. We all make mistakes, and that is completely normal. I always tell my employees that I love mistakes because they show me that the employee is trying and not giving up. The key is simply not to make the same mistake twice. This is the crux of leadership. Be proud of your mistakes and embrace your vulnerabilities as part of your journey.

I have made plenty of mistakes in both my personal and professional life, but instead of dwelling on them, I look for the silver lining and the lesson within each situation. Doing this not only makes us better leaders; it also helps us become more resilient and grounded in our confidence.

Finally, you must be kind to yourself and trust your intuition. We talked earlier about negative self-talk, but now, it is time to focus on the positive. The little voice in your head that often leads you to question yourself can also have a positive impact on your confidence when managed intentionally. We have all been there—those awkward moments when you say the wrong thing or go in for a hug when the other person extends a handshake. It feels uncomfortable, and the more we dwell on it, the louder that inner critic becomes.

We must be conscious of that voice and be intentional in our response to it. Challenge and reframe negative or limiting beliefs by focusing on your strengths and turning self-criticism into constructive reflection. This is how you build a habit of positive self-talk that strengthens your confidence from the inside out. It helps you build trust within yourself instead of creating doubt. This is when you know you are building confidence, and it is working. You begin to develop the ability to distinguish between fear and intuition under pressure, allowing you to navigate chaos with clarity and confidence.

You are now prepared to embrace future shifts in your mindset as you continue to transition from fearing the unknown to viewing it as a growth opportunity. You are now becoming a resilient and adaptable leader, equipped with practical tools to handle the challenges that life throws your way. However, it's important at this stage that we do not get ahead of ourselves and ride off into the sunset! The work is not done yet. We need to nurture this new skill and perfect it.

The first step is fully embracing a growth mindset and using it to its full extent, acknowledging that your skills and abilities always need refining, by finding growth in every win and every failure. It is not just about finding the silver lining in failure. What about when you succeed? Do you slam the laptop shut, give a high five, or take your "attaboy" and move on? No. Celebrate the win, absolutely, but when the dust settles, take time to reflect. Look for opportunities where you can improve, or approach things differently next time. Perfection does not exist, and there is always room for growth. We need to live in that continuous cycle of winning, improving, and winning again.

Start by setting small, achievable goals. We need to work toward greatness, and this is how we get there. I love the acronym, SMART goals, which stands for specific, measurable, achievable, relevant, and time-bound. These principles are essential to the goal-setting process and serve as the foundation for steady, sustainable progress. This is how we cultivate the feedback loop we discussed earlier—the cycle of constant improvement and growth.

The best part is that this loop applies to both our successes and our failures in life. Trust me, once you begin this process, you will find yourself motivated to take on bigger challenges. It is only up from here.

Use your support system to strengthen this commitment. Do not go at it alone. Surround yourself with a village of supportive individuals who understand your vision and will help you reach your destination. These may be family, friends, peers, or mentors who can offer guidance and provide encouragement during difficult times. This is your network. And if you do not have one yet, do not worry, we will cover practical tips later in the book on how to build one.

Our last point here is to stay healthy. People often underestimate the connection between physical and mental health and how deeply it affects overall well-being. By maintaining a healthy lifestyle, you strengthen your resilience and enhance your ability to handle the mental strain that comes with adapting to different environments. This also elevates your sense of self-worth, which is a vital part of building confidence and sustaining long-term success as a leader. Remember, leadership is not just about leading others; it starts with taking care of yourself first.

PART III
LEADING FROM WITHIN

*Transforming Confidence into
Authentic Influence*

The Leadership Legacy

The second half of this book laid the foundation, exploring how perseverance, authenticity, and credibility form the framework of thought leadership. We began with mindset and habits, moved through consistency and values, and discovered how influence grows from the inside out.

Now, it is time to move from understanding to application. In the chapters ahead, we will go beyond personal growth and step into strategic leadership, where credibility becomes influence, innovation drives relevance, and confidence becomes the engine of impact.

Part III is about legacy. It is about leading from within and translating experience into wisdom and influence into service. As we move forward, we will explore how authentic storytelling, meaningful collaboration, and ethical influence transform personal success into enduring impact—the hallmark of every great leader.

Chapter 7

Storytelling as a Leadership Tool

"Those who tell the stories rule the world." – Plato

When we discuss the value of leadership, it is essential to understand the tools we have at our disposal to enhance our impact on those we serve. This is a crucial aspect of thought leadership because influence is only meaningful when it drives action. To make a lasting impression, whether we are sharing a message, launching an initiative, or inspiring change, we must learn to leverage one of the most powerful tools available to any leader: the art of storytelling. Storytelling is a transformative leadership tool that builds authentic connections, simplifies complex ideas, and inspires others. It engages their emotions and making messages more memorable. This is the goal and the crux of this part of our journey.

As thought leaders, we use this strategy to establish credibility, demonstrate expertise, and inspire action. But how does this function as a leadership tool? That is an interesting question and one that took me years to fully understand. Fortunately for you, I am going to save you the time and explain the value of this strategy as a leadership tool.

At first, this was something I was not good at, and was very reluctant to do, especially in professional environments. Do not get me wrong, it was easy to use stories to convey a message or lesson to my friends or family. But in the workplace, I froze. I second-guessed the validity and relevance of my story. Would they care? Does it make sense? Am I being long-winded? These were all questions that ran through my mind at just the thought of telling a story to a colleague or peer. This constant self-doubt kept me from recognizing the true power of storytelling until I finally discovered its inherent value. It was more than just a prop to support the main point; it was a powerful tool that, when used intentionally, helped shape my career in ways I could never have imagined.

Storytelling helps build connection and trust with your audience. It makes you human and validates the points you are trying to make, by tying them to real-world experiences. It truly matters, and you may be surprised by how many people find stories engaging. They help others understand complex ideas by providing context and relatability. I encourage you to draw upon your lived experiences and use the art of storytelling to evoke empathy and a sense of shared understanding. Challenge yourself to connect with your audience on a deeper level by sharing the experiences that shaped the person and leader you are today, especially when driving home an important point.

Inspire and motivate your audience by framing your vision through a compelling narrative that draws them in, captivates their attention, and moves them to act. As leaders, we want to motivate our teams, peers, and colleagues to work towards a common purpose, by using your story as a roadmap for our journey. We do not just tell stories to tell stories; they must have a genuine purpose and add value to those we tell them to.

This is the foundation of the communication strategy we are building. Leaders communicate vision and values through stories, transforming abstract ideas into relatable experiences. This approach brings concepts to life and turns theory into action. It makes the "why" more relatable and helps it evolve into what I call the RR (relevant and resonant). When your message is both relevant and resonates with your audience, it becomes far more impactful and memorable.

Our stories are powerful tools, but only when they demonstrate certain qualities that make them credible to the audience. Make your stories authentic and genuine. Avoid the trap of crafting exaggerated or unrealistic stories, because your audience will see through them within minutes of your presentation. Your story needs to come from the heart and reflect your genuine passion for the topic or the action you are advocating for.

Every story should have a clear purpose. Before you tell it, ask yourself: what is the reason I am sharing this story, and does it align with my overall message? Stay off the tangent train and remain focused. We all have the tendency to wander off course when telling stories, but as leaders, we must learn to recognize this behavior and redirect ourselves. In this sense, we are once again becoming change agents—only this time, the change begins within us.

But I would be remiss not to highlight the one element that ties all of this together and makes it truly work—emotional resonance. This is something I want you to focus on and develop as a leader. You need the ability to evoke emotion in your audience. Do this with every story you tell by using vivid, descriptive language that paints a clear picture. The right context draws your audience into the experience of the story, creating a powerful emotional connection that makes your message unforgettable.

This is the cornerstone of authentic leadership. Authentic leaders are genuine and transparent. They earn the trust of their audience through honesty and consistency. As we discussed earlier in the book, they foster a heightened sense of psychological safety, creating environments where others feel valued, heard, and empowered to contribute.

So, how does this connect to storytelling? What turns authenticity from a phrase into an action? The answer is simple: we continue building on the principles we have already discussed. Being authentic means sharing your stories in a genuine and vulnerable way. Use stories that reveal the person behind the professional, by sharing your experiences, struggles, and successes. And do not forget to acknowledge your mistakes within those stories. We have said this before, but it bears repeating: do not only tell the good. Use your failures as teaching moments. Let them humanize you and show your audience that growth comes from imperfection.

Now that you understand the importance of storytelling as a leadership tool and its value to us as thought leaders, we need to discuss how to use it effectively. Yes, use personal anecdotes. Be authentic and vulnerable. Bring your concepts to life by humanizing them. That has been the essence of our discussion so far. But now, it is time to go deeper. I want to help you become an impact player.

When you tell your stories, you must deliver them with authority and confidence because you are the subject matter expert in your field. And never, and I mean never, forget to land the plane. This is one of the most common mistakes I see leaders, both new and seasoned, make during their speaking engagements. They forget the final punch—the clear takeaway that empowers the audience to act or view the world differently. This is your call to action—or CTA.

It brings me back to an experience early in my career when I attended a company meeting where the CEO of a major technology company gave an inspiring speech about the organization's vision and goals. But one problem: they never landed the plane. Most of us walked into that room excited and motivated but left confused and unsure of what to do next. That is exactly what I want to help you avoid. In this section, we are going to focus on giving you the tools and structure needed to consistently land the plane by delivering clear, actionable, and memorable messages that leave a lasting impact on your audience.

Before we get to what it takes to deliver clear takeaways to your audience, we must start with the message and work our way backwards.

When you begin crafting your story and thinking about why it matters, you must start with the "why" and the "I." This is the first step of the process and, honestly, one of the most important. It is where you establish your credibility, by sharing your unique perspective in a genuine way that connects your personal experience with your audience. You need to create a bridge between yourself and the audience to capture their attention and earn their trust before moving toward the call to action.

How can you expect someone to invest time in listening or energy in following your advice if you do not have credibility? This is the moment to do it in a big way. Be vulnerable and showcase your transformation to your audience. Use your journey as a tool to craft an authentic and compelling narrative. Start with the "before," introduce the disruption that represents the challenge or turning point, reveal the struggle, and then close with the "after," sharing the lessons and insights you gained along the way. Using this structure creates an emotional connection that makes your story powerful, relatable, and memorable.

But once again, be vulnerable with your story. Do not sugarcoat or omit any of the details from your audience—this is where credibility is built. Use your emotions and pain to your advantage. Show your passion by varying your tone and using your body language intentionally. When your audience hears the passion in your voice and feels the emotion behind your words, whether it is frustration, excitement, or pain, you create empathy and connection. This is what makes your story relatable and brings it to life.

I remember giving a motivational speech to a group of young men about the dangers of social media and its impact on youth. You can imagine how important I wanted this message to be for them. At first, they ignored me, scrolling through their phones and barely paying attention. But when I began sharing a story about how people have ruined their lives by being glued to their phones and neglecting their education, something changed.

I spoke with conviction, using my own experiences as the backdrop, and I noticed the room shift. They became quiet, listening intently. The more vulnerable I became, the more I had their attention. They were no longer just hearing my words; they were feeling them.

Now, it is time to land the plane. This is always my favorite part of the process. It is something we cannot reach without giving enough context, but if we take too long to get there, we risk losing our audience. We have all sat through a presentation with a long-winded speaker who delays getting to the point, only to deliver an ending that falls flat.

When I spoke to those young men, I made sure to deliver a powerful closing message. I landed the plane with a strong call to action: use your phone less and be more present in real life. But that alone was not enough. I needed to tell them how. I had to leave them with clear, actionable takeaways that they could immediately put into practice.

Ultimately, that is the goal of any great message: to leave your audience inspired, and to challenge their perspective, helping them see the issue or opportunity in a new light.

These are the points you need to take into consideration when building your narrative. So, put them into action, and you will see that the narrative you build will be powerful and long-lasting. When I begin writing my narratives, I use the 5 Cs to make sure that I cover all the different points when crafting the message. It is extremely intuitive, but often overlooked, so we are going to cover it quickly but thoroughly. If you have heard of it, consider this a review; if you haven't, you are about to gain a new tool.

First, we must build context before moving to the problem. Give some background on yourself and the situation. This is where you set the stage, by explaining why and how the issue has personally impacted you. Then, introduce the challenge. Clearly define the problem, but do not just state it; explain it. Be detailed and make it engaging by using those vivid descriptions we discussed earlier to help your audience visualize it.

This is the climax of your story; the moment when your audience should be leaning in, fully engaged, and eager to hear what happens next. That is how you know you are doing it right. I often take a brief pause to look around the room, and in that silence, I can tell if I have them hooked.

And then, guess what? You land the plane with a powerful punch and a clear call to action. Always conclude your story in a way that inspires and motivates your audience. If you do not, you are wasting both their time and yours.

An addition that is not necessary but helpful is the use of suspense. Think of this as a personal movie. Build tension and anticipation to keep your audience engaged. Do not be afraid to embellish a little. This is part of the storytelling process, and it is perfectly fine to dramatize your story, as long as you do not exaggerate the main point. A memorable moment of suspense or a touch of humor never hurts; it only strengthens your story and makes it more impactful.

Your narratives are going to do more than tell a story; they are going to inspire action and build trust with your audience. This is what makes storytelling such a compelling and powerful tool for us as leaders. It is our sword in battle; the instrument we use to lead, motivate, and rally our teams toward a shared vision.

At its core, storytelling transforms communication from transactional to transformational. It takes a simple recommendation and elevates it into a powerful playbook for action—a framework that not only informs but also inspires. When done well, your story becomes more than a message; it becomes a movement that others can see themselves in, believe in, and act upon.

We must weave storytelling into our daily activities to emphasize key points, convey strategy, and inspire action. It is more than a communication style; it is part of the culture of leadership itself. Storytelling does not have to be long or dramatic to be effective. Sometimes, short and simple examples can be just as powerful. The key is using the right story at the right moment to reinforce the message and add value.

However, I would never encourage you to use stories carelessly. Doing so can waste time and frustrate your peers or colleagues. The real skill lies in recognizing the right opportunities and knowing when to wield your sword. When you master timing and purpose, you inherit the power of storytelling as a leadership strategy.

Always stay true to the purpose behind your story. There is a simple hierarchy framework that helps us stay focused on why we tell stories in the first place. The goal is to inform, influence, and inspire our audience. When you think about telling a story, use these three points as your guide; they will help you stay relevant, intentional, and impactful every single time.

Why do we use storytelling to inform? Because it simplifies complex ideas and makes them easily digestible for your audience. As a professor of management, I can tell you that this is my go-to tool with my students. It allows me to bring abstract or archaic concepts to life and make them understandable. But that is just the beginning of storytelling's power in leadership.

When we want to influence, storytelling goes even further. It allows us to take hold of our audience's attention, emphasizing key points and creating a sense of urgency that motivates action. This is how we gain buy-in, foster alignment, and shape perspectives on critical issues. Think about how political leaders use this technique. They rely on strong, vivid language to describe the challenges facing society, and the consequences of inaction. Their stories not only influence opinions but also inspire people to act.

That inspiration is the final and most powerful layer of storytelling. It is what transforms belief into behavior. It is what creates long-term commitment and helps others navigate inconvenience or adversity while remaining steadfast to the goal.

The best part of mastering this process is that its impact extends far beyond you. It carries over to your audience, colleagues, and peers. Your stories hold power over time, across challenges, and through barriers of politics, race, and gender. Storytelling becomes a cultural driver that reinforces organizational values and purpose.

Think of it like an old workplace folklore—the story of one legendary employee that gets passed down from generation to generation because it perfectly embodies the organization's core values. That is the ripple effect of storytelling; it creates a domino effect throughout your organization. It goes beyond your personal leadership. It is about how you use your voice and your story to spark long-lasting action that reaches beyond your immediate audience. This is how you build alignment, emotional connection, and shared purpose. This is how you create real, lasting impact.

Once you start to see the impact of your work and the fruits of your labor paying off, take the time to celebrate. You have earned it. But once the celebration is over, it is time to pause and evaluate yourself. This is where you step back into the role of the self-aware leader we talked about earlier. Reflection is key to growth and continued impact.

There is no single set of questions that fits every situation, but here are a few that have worked wonders for me over the years:
- Did it change perception or behavior?
- Did it increase engagement or clarity?
- Did it create shared ownership of the mission?

These simple but powerful questions help you gauge whether your message resonated and whether your leadership truly inspired transformation.

Your Story Is Your Legacy

Your story is more than communication; it is your leadership legacy. When wielded with purpose and authenticity, storytelling becomes a force that amplifies influence, builds connection, and defines how you will be remembered. Our stories outlive our titles and accomplishments. They shape how others experience our leadership and what they carry forward long after our work is done.

Your narrative is not just an autobiography; it is a leadership asset. Through consistency and authenticity, your story becomes your brand, humanizing your voice across every platform where you lead, speak, and serve. In the end, our legacy is written not only in what we achieved, but in how others remember the way we made them feel and the way we inspired them to act.

Chapter 8

Leveraging Networks and Collaboration

"Alone we can do so little; together we can do so much."
– Helen Keller

We are now stepping fully into the world as leaders. We have made tremendous strides in building our arsenal of tools necessary to become, in my opinion, world-renowned thought leaders over the past several chapters. But now, it is time to build our audience. Remember earlier when we discussed the importance of a network? This is where that concept comes full circle.

We are going to explore how to build a strong network and, more importantly, how to use it strategically to our advantage. Because the truth is, no one leads alone. Every great leader understands the power of collaboration and the value of allies who can support, amplify, and advance a shared vision.

It is our social capital, and it is a powerful asset that every leader must learn to leverage. This is what extends a leader's influence beyond formal authority, providing greater visibility, access to opportunities, and the ability to mobilize networks for collective success. But before we get too far ahead of ourselves, let's define this concept. Social capital is an intangible asset that leaders develop over time through intentional interactions, trust building, and meaningful engagement within their network.

Unintentionally, this is where many professionals stumble in their leadership journey at one point or another, myself included. Failing to recognize or appreciate the power of our network has been the downfall of many great leaders. The good news is that you do not have to share that fate, and neither did I. In this section, we are going to discuss strategies that will help you harness the power of your network and use it as a strategic tool to expand your influence and advance your leadership impact.

To unlock this power, we must start by focusing on three key elements: our relationships, our reputation, and the results we deliver. These are the pillars that shape how others perceive our leadership and determine the reach of our influence. The question then becomes: how can we operationalize these elements to our advantage and use them to strengthen our impact?

Let's start with relationships—one of the most important aspects of leadership. Building authentic connections with peers, colleagues, and professionals both inside and outside of your immediate network is essential. But it cannot stop there. True growth happens when you expand your circle beyond your industry. Your knowledge, lived experiences, and wisdom hold tremendous value across disciplines and sectors in ways you may not even realize. The real challenge lies in making that value visible and accessible to others.

This is where your reputation comes into play as a powerful asset that drives both visibility and accessibility. Your reputation is the respect and credibility you have earned as a leader over the course of your career, and it fuels the growth of others within your professional network. When you actively engage and connect with people in your network, you are doing far more than sending a friend request or making small talk. You are positioning yourself as a connector who bridges individuals, ideas, and opportunities that can benefit one another.

This makes you a strategic hub that strengthens your influence. Your reputation is what inspires trust, prompts others to extend favors, and gives you the bargaining power essential to the timeless exchange system that leaders use behind the scenes to make deals, build alliances, and shape decisions.

The results of these actions hold the key to your power. I know it sounds a bit ironic, doesn't it? Your power in networking is directly derived from how effectively you build and nurture relationships with your peers. The stronger your connections and the more value you bring to those relationships, the greater your influence becomes.

There are, however, a few ways to enhance your results and create a bigger impact. One of the most effective ways is to invest with intention, focusing on quality over quantity when building relationships. Your connections with colleagues and mentors, both inside and outside your industry, need to be nurtured consistently. The simplest way to do this is by making time for them: schedule a quick coffee, lunch, or even a short virtual chat. This helps ensure that your relationships remain authentic and genuine.

It can be distasteful to only reach out when you need something, so make it a best practice to check in periodically. A thoughtful email, a brief phone call, or a simple note to acknowledge someone's recent accomplishment goes a long way in maintaining meaningful, long-lasting connections.

It is also important to practice reciprocity. In our daily lives, we should never expect an immediate return on our generosity or investment. When you offer support, share advice, or create opportunities for others, you build goodwill and trust over time. This is what people notice, and it strengthens your reputation as a reliable and trustworthy leader who contributes without expectation and leads through genuine service.

The goal of practicing the 3Rs of Relationships, Reputation, and Results is to pair this strategy with strong listening skills. Listen first and ask second. Pay close attention to the needs and challenges of others before stepping in to offer assistance. This is a crucial step in building genuine networks, which are grounded in the principle of helping others through mutually beneficial relationships.

Build your connections on authenticity and sincerity. We have emphasized these two qualities repeatedly throughout this book for a reason. They are not optional; they are essential. You must practice them daily and make them a part of your personal core values. Long-lasting connections are built on trust, honesty, and genuine intent.

When people sense your authenticity, they are far more likely to stay connected, collaborate, and support your leadership journey. In the end, social capital is what transforms connection into collaboration, and collaboration into collective success. It's not about who you know, but how you nurture what you know through others. The leaders who master this don't just build networks; they build communities that outlast them.

These communities are selective in nature; not everyone is granted entry into the kingdom. Only high-value relationships exist within this ecosystem, adding intrinsic worth to our professional lives. You will recognize these relationships because they are balanced. Giving and receiving are met with mutual flexibility, respect, and accommodation. In these relationships, no one feels used or taken advantage of in the name of gaining benefits.

Now, to be clear, there will be times when someone reaches out to you, or you reach out to them, for a specific favor or opportunity. That is perfectly normal. The key, however, lies in maintaining a balanced approach over time. When both parties invest in and benefit from the relationship, it evolves into a sustainable and mutually rewarding connection. You become partners rather than just colleagues, peers, or mentors, united by a shared outcome.

In these relationships, you are open and transparent with your thoughts and feedback. It is not about manipulation, but about honesty and genuine communication. This space is meant to be a place of safety and trust, not a political arena. You respect and value each other's time, never taking it for granted. Every conversation, every shared insight, and every moment of collaboration is a voluntary act of mutual growth—an investment of precious time that adds real value to both lives.

This is where you develop what I like to call the platinum experience in networking. It goes beyond the golden rule of treating others as you want to be treated. Instead, it focuses on understanding and responding to the unique needs and wants of others, using that awareness as the foundation of the relationship. By doing so, you create meaningful, personalized connections that show genuine care and respect, elevating your network from transactional to transformational.

These relationships form the foundation for developing cross-industry strategic partnerships that expand your professional network, enhance your skillset, and strengthen your reputation. When you collaborate with professionals from different fields, you gain access to new ideas, diverse problem-solving approaches, and broader perspectives. This not only fuels innovation, but also gives you a distinct competitive advantage within your industry.

It also gives you access to their audience, which can expand your reach dramatically. When someone likes or comments on your post on LinkedIn or shares your story on Instagram, your ideas and insights are introduced to people who may never have discovered you otherwise. This is one of the most powerful aspects of building a strong network.

I remember when I first started sharing my ideas online, I struggled to expand my network. I would meet people at events, but the connections rarely lasted beyond the room. It felt like my reach ended the moment I walked out the door. Everything changed when I began consistently posting meaningful, relevant content that resonated with my audience. Slowly but surely, people started sending connection requests and following my work. New opportunities began to emerge, and for the first time, I could see my influence growing, and my network maturing in real time.

This was just one of the benefits of expanding my network. The second major outcome was that it broadened my knowledge and helped me strengthen my critical thinking skills, allowing me to create more innovative solutions. The diverse perspectives I encountered played a crucial role in shaping this growth. When you collaborate with people from different industries and backgrounds, you break free from siloed thinking and begin developing higher-order reasoning. These new insights encourage you to approach challenges from multiple angles, resulting in more creative and well-rounded solutions.

The by-product of this phenomenon is accelerated learning. When you combine insights from a variety of perspectives, you naturally put yourself in an environment where learning becomes faster and deeper. You begin to pick up techniques, strategies, and best practices more quickly than you could on your own. This ties directly back to the earlier point about being a lifelong learner; this is where you see the payoff of that mindset in action.

It is also the perfect opportunity not only to acquire knowledge, but to share it in true thought leadership fashion. Knowledge sharing is one of the most powerful abilities we possess as human beings. In its simplest form, it is how information was exchanged long before the world discovered tools like ChatGPT. It is through this exchange that ideas flourish and collaborators create well-rounded, enriching experiences together.

If you execute this effectively, it will transform how you are perceived in your field. You move from simply being knowledgeable to being seen as a trusted authority who contributes to the growth of others, while advancing the collective understanding of your industry. This demonstrates your expertise, strengthens your credibility and shows that you are adaptable and capable of working with a diverse community of professionals. These are essential leadership traits, and when consistently displayed, they naturally command respect and reinforce your standing within your field.

I can imagine the next burning question is: how do you do this? The answer is quite straightforward; it's not rocket science. Here are a few practical ways to get started:

- **Interviews:** Conduct or participate in interviews (written, audio, or video) with experts outside your field to share new knowledge with your audience.
- **Joint webinars or workshops:** Co-host a digital event with a complementary partner to combine your expertise and cross-promote to each other's audiences.
- **Guest posts:** Write an article for another professional's blog or invite a cross-industry colleague to post on yours. This helps you reach a fresh audience and introduces new perspectives.
- **Social media takeovers:** Partner with another professional and take over each other's social media accounts for a day to showcase your work, share insights, and engage with new audiences.
- **Joint product creation:** Team up with a partner to create a new e-book, course, or digital product that leverages both of your strengths and provides mutual value to your audiences.

These strategies not only expand your network, but also deepen your credibility and influence across industries. However, it is important not to let your pursuit of networking overshadow or distract you from the value of mentorship and shared learning. Mentorship is another powerful dyadic relationship, similar to networking, where both the mentor and mentee benefit from mutual growth and exchange.

In the next section, we are going to explore this complex relationship from both perspectives (the mentor and the mentee) to build context around its value and help you clearly distinguish it from traditional networking. Understanding this distinction will allow you to approach mentorship intentionally and harness its full potential for personal and professional development.

Being a mentor is one of the most rewarding experiences you can have as a leader. It is an opportunity to pay it forward and pour into the cup of a junior leader who can benefit from your guidance and wisdom. The time to give back is now.

Mentorship offers more benefits than simply being seen as a role model. It helps you develop your coaching and active listening skills, while also giving you valuable practice in providing effective feedback and navigating challenging situations with diplomacy. Through mentoring, you not only shape others; you refine your own leadership in the process.

It helps you find a renewed sense of purpose in life. I remember when I first joined the 5000 Role Models of Excellence Project. I became a mentor to young men in middle and high school. It was a terrifying experience at first, to say the least. But I applied the practices we discussed earlier in this book and turned that challenge into an opportunity to sharpen my skills.

It is safe to say that I eventually persevered, but the main point I want to make here is that the experience helped me develop a new sense of purpose in my life.

I had served as a mentor in a professional capacity many times before, but this experience was different. It was humbling. It helped me reconnect with my true passion, education, and mentorship. That is when I realized that what fulfilled me was helping others succeed and overcome adversity. That sense of purpose reignited my drive and reminded me that leadership is not just about achievement; it is about impact.

Being a mentor exposed me to so many different perspectives that it expanded my professional paradigm to new horizons. It challenged my way of thinking and pushed me to broaden my perspective, by exploring unfamiliar concepts and ideas. It also helped me clarify my own understanding of various subjects, and strengthen my overall knowledge. Ultimately, teaching others solidifies your mastery of the topic and reinforces your expertise, consequently making you a stronger subject matter expert. It also benefits the mentee, who is the most important person in this relationship. They are the reason you are a leader, and the reason you chose to become a mentor. They are who you serve.

Let's discuss why mentorship is so important for the mentee. For them, shared learning offers a guided and accelerated path to personal and professional development. As mentors, we provide a safe space for our mentees to be vulnerable and to grow. It is a space where they can receive honest, unbiased, and nonjudgmental feedback. Here, they can openly discuss their insecurities, challenges, and aspirations with someone they trust, who can help them navigate uncertainty with clarity and confidence.

The feedback we offer our mentees gives them the ability to step outside themselves and view their situation from an outside perspective. It allows them to reflect more objectively, identify blind spots, and recognize both their strengths and areas for improvement. This process of guided self-awareness helps them grow into more confident, capable, and intentional professionals. They leave us with a heightened level of self-awareness, which, honestly, is one of our main goals as mentors.

Our purpose is not only to give advice, though that is certainly important, but to help them build confidence, motivation, and communication skills. We want to help them develop personal goals, expand their perspectives, and see things from new angles. When we do this correctly, something special happens. We witness their transformation. They begin to develop genuine self-confidence and resilience. They become active listeners, capable of clearly and effectively articulating their opinions and ideas. Most importantly, they become accountable, not to others, but to themselves, taking full ownership of their actions and progress toward achieving their goals.

Being a mentor is more than building relationships or helping someone reach their goals and aspirations. It is about laying the foundation for strategic alliances. This is how you focus on building and nurturing meaningful relationships with individuals and groups who possess complementary strengths and can help expand your reach. This is where you harness the power of networking and collaboration as a strategic tool to support your leadership growth and influence.

As an introvert, I can tell you that this was one component of leadership that I struggled with early in my career and continue to refine as a senior leader in my field. But little by little, I have witnessed the tremendous impact of having a strong network and developing strategic alliances. Over the years, I have been fortunate to speak at several professional conferences in my formal capacity as a leader, as well as in informal settings as a community advocate at high schools and local events.

However, let me be clear, this is not about relying solely on your network. You must be qualified and bring something of value to the table for this complex relationship to work. One common pitfall I have seen is professionals who depend too heavily on their network without establishing their own credibility or expertise. A strong network can open doors, but only your competence and authenticity will keep them open. To move from mentorship to strategic alliance, you must embody the fundamental principles that serve as the pillars of strong, lasting partnerships.

For starters, you must intentionally and deliberately earn trust from your audience and peers. This means being consistent, dependable, and honest in your actions. Always follow through on your commitments, no matter how small they may seem. Trust is built through repetition and reliability over time.

It is also essential to be a person of character—a true representation of who you claim to be. Your authenticity must align with your words and actions. No more false advertisement or image management. People can sense when someone is genuine, and they can sense when someone is not. The goal is to embody integrity so that others know they can rely on you, not because of your title or reputation, but because your behavior proves it.

Secondly, you must consistently demonstrate your credibility and level of expertise. You are an expert. It is time to drop the imposter syndrome and step fully into your light, showing the world who you truly are. This is the foundation of your alliances. Your peers and colleagues want to know that they are working with someone who is not only honest but competent. They need to trust that the advice and guidance you provide are rooted in experience, knowledge, and sound judgment.

Finally, engage with empathy when nurturing these relationships. This is where you embrace your altruistic self by prioritizing the mutual benefit of the partnership. Take the time to understand the goals, motivations, and challenges of those you work with. Then collaborate to create win-win scenarios that foster growth and success for everyone involved. This approach not only strengthens your alliances, but also amplifies your influence as a leader who uplifts others. Remember, thought leadership thrives within a collaborative ecosystem. The relationships you build will multiply your reach, expand your credibility, and amplify your lasting impact. As you move forward, remember that leadership is not built in isolation. It is shaped through empathy, collaboration, and the shared pursuit of purpose. Every connection you make is another step toward the legacy you are building.

Chapter 9

Ethical Influence in a Complex World

"Integrity is doing the right thing, even when no one is watching."
– C.S. Lewis

We are now at an interesting juncture in our thought leadership journey. This is the moment when we examine how to ethically use our newly established influence. This is a critical topic and one that would have been remiss to overlook before transitioning to the final part of this book. It represents the culmination of all the lessons, wisdom, and insights we have gathered along the way.

Have you ever heard the phrase, "With great power comes great responsibility"? You have probably heard it in a movie, but guess what? It is real, and it applies right here, right now. As thought leaders, our influence carries weight, and how we choose to use it defines not only our legacy, but the impact we leave on others.

When we talk about ethics, what do we really mean? How can influence be used unethically? And what safeguards can we put in place to ensure we use it correctly every single time? These are just a few of the questions I am often asked when consulting, and I chose them for a reason. They are among the most important and consistent questions I receive.

These questions get to the heart of what it means to lead responsibly. Influence, when used ethically, can inspire and drive meaningful change. But when misused, it can manipulate, mislead, and erode trust. Understanding this balance is what separates great leaders from self-serving ones.

Ethical influence hinges on your intent and the methods you use to shape outcomes. In simple terms, the question becomes: are you striving for a win-win or a win-lose? Are you creating mutual value, or are you the only one benefiting from the relationship? The moment your influence shifts from collaboration to self-interest, you begin to drift away from the principles of ethical leadership. This is where reflection, self-awareness, and purpose must take center stage to ensure that your influence continues to empower rather than exploit.

Having the right intentions is the most important aspect of leading with ethics. You must do things for the right reasons for them to have a lasting impact. It is not uncommon to have cynical tendencies. It is human nature and instinct. But if we can proactively recognize them and change this behavior, we will be empowered to move with the correct intent to identify mutual benefit and understanding.

Sometimes, it is not as obvious as you might think, but I can guarantee you that if you look hard enough, you will find the silver lining. We also need to be self-aware and examine the methodology we are using to gain this influence. Are we using logical arguments, credible evidence, and balanced emotional appeals? Or are we basing our influence on half-information and lies?

Be open and transparent with your colleagues. This is one of the most powerful ways to build trust. When you share your sources, explain your methodology, and acknowledge any potential biases, to build transparency, your credibility increases because it shows you have nothing to hide.

Encourage feedback from your audience and make them feel comfortable asking questions. This open dialogue empowers them to seek clarity and make informed decisions using their own free will. These tactics form the foundation of persuasion, which is an ethical approach to influence.

Now, what about unethical means of influence, better known as manipulation? This is a dangerous area, and I strongly warn you never to participate in it when you are in a position of leadership. Manipulation will eventually undermine everything you have worked so hard to build. I can promise you that.

When you compare manipulation to persuasion, the red flags become clear. Manipulation centers on the leader's self-interest, often at the expense of others. A manipulative leader provides distorted or misleading information to serve a private agenda, whether that agenda is publicity, votes, or influencing purchasing behavior. It is cynical and self-serving, and it preys on vulnerability. That is why populations with limited access to education or resources are especially at risk of this kind of abuse.

Stay transparent, stay honest, and always ask yourself if the outcome you seek benefits others as well as yourself. If it does not, rethink the approach. Ethical influence builds trust and endures. Manipulation corrodes trust and destroys legacy. It is a polarized concept, especially when tactics like guilt, deceit, or emotional pressure are used to gain control or influence. What inevitably follows is a breakdown in transparency, where communication becomes performative rather than purposeful, and trust erodes beyond repair.

In today's world, where propaganda is widespread and easily accessible through social media and digital platforms, it is imperative that we remain conscious of how we use our influence. Leadership in the digital age comes with an even greater responsibility to ensure that our words, actions, and platforms are not weaponized or used to mislead others. Instead, we must model integrity and use our voices to inform, uplift, and inspire positive change.

Leadership in the era of misinformation is built on trust and transparency. That is why we have spent so much time dialing in on ethical influence. Full disclosure, this section may feel a bit familiar at first, but it is not redundant. We are going to explore these two concepts in greater detail because they are the cornerstone of ethical influence. Stay with me as we land this plane and help you become the ethically aware thought leader we know you can be.

Trust is one of the most important characteristics that a leader can possess in the era of misinformation. This is the guiding light that helps your audience navigate this tumultuous environment. So, communicate effectively and proactively. Misinformation thrives in a vacuum! The easiest way to fight this is to deliver clear and accurate information. It is best to anticipate any questions and get as much information as you can to address them early before falsehood can begin to develop.

It is also important to own up to your mistakes in a timely manner. Do not wait. A mistake is a mistake, and all you can do is acknowledge it and move forward. The motto at my church says it best: "No Perfect People Allowed." When you demonstrate that you are willing to take responsibility publicly, you step into a higher realm of leadership where truth outweighs ego.

Once you reach this level, it becomes easier to lead with evidence. You move away from relying solely on anecdotes and focus instead on facts when making critical decisions. It is equally important to admit what you do not know and to have the courage to make decisions based on data, even when information is limited. To do this effectively, you must surround yourself with people who know what they are talking about; your subject matter experts. These individuals will serve as your advisors, trusted confidants, and amplifiers of your message, helping you extend your influence and strengthen your leadership credibility.

But remember, it is not all about you. As a leader, you must consider your team and foster an environment that promotes a culture of truth-seeking and critical thinking. We must empower our teams by encouraging digital literacy and basic research skills. Teach them how to recognize and respond to misinformation effectively.

It is more than just receiving information and reacting to it; we have to become analytical. Teach your team to pause and evaluate the quality of information before sharing it. Ensure that communication is accurate, concise, and credible. Remember the game of telephone we played as children? Well, we are not playing that here. It is essential to relay information exactly as it was shared. If something is unclear or incomplete, avoid the temptation to fill in the blanks, and instead, refer others back to the original source for clarity. This simple habit builds trust, accuracy, and integrity in every layer of your organization.

This is part of practicing personal social responsibility in leadership. It is the process of considering the broader impact of your actions on society and ultimately working toward the greater good. Leadership extends beyond personal or organizational success; it involves ensuring that your influence contributes positively to the world around you. It is our civic and moral duty to consider this impact. Leadership goes beyond self. You are entrusted with great power, which is the impact you make on the general welfare of your community with your influence. You use this influence in a manner that aligns with your core values and demonstrates integrity in your actions.

These are the tools we can use to navigate ethical dilemmas, especially when it comes to innovation and communication. As thought leaders, we play a critical role in shaping industry standards and promoting responsible practices that balance progress with integrity. However, being at the forefront of innovation also comes with heightened responsibility. You are expected to create, experiment, and share new ideas, but how do you do this without compromising your values or crossing ethical boundaries? The answer lies in intentionality. You must innovate with purpose, ensuring that every new idea, process, or technology serves the greater good and aligns with your ethical framework.

When you are an innovative leader, you will often encounter challenges that test your ethical compass. There are countless issues that could arise, far too many to cover here, but we can address some of the most common ones and explore strategies to navigate them effectively. The goal is not to provide a one-size-fits-all guide, but to equip you with practical tools and frameworks that you can adapt to your unique circumstances as a leader.

One of the most common challenges we face as leaders today involves data and privacy concerns related to technology. In the 21st century, nearly every technological deployment exposes our organizations to some level of risk, especially with the amount of Personally Protected Information (PPI) we collect both directly and indirectly. As leaders, we must acknowledge these risks and confront them head-on, maintaining transparency in how we collect, store, and disseminate information.

It is our responsibility to model and champion ethical behavior in both our actions and our words, setting the standard for integrity and accountability as thought leaders. Have you ever heard the saying, "It's not about what you do when someone is looking that makes you a leader; it's what you do when people are not looking"? This is where the real challenge comes in for you as a leader within your organization. There will be moments when you are required to navigate conflicts between your personal values and your professional obligations.

These situations test your integrity, your decision-making, and your ability to uphold ethical standards even when no one is watching. They are the defining moments that separate leaders who simply hold authority from those who truly embody leadership.

I remember a situation earlier in my career when I was presenting an executive update to my company's Board of Directors on the status of a major project. Prior to the meeting, the vendor asked me to highlight only the positive aspects of the project and downplay the negatives. I initially declined the request. But shortly after, I received a phone call from a senior leader who pressured me to comply, insisting that a positive report was necessary to secure additional funding. This was not the first time my personal values conflicted with my professional obligations, but it was the first time I was asked to use my influence to guide others' decisions based on misguided information.

This was a critical moment in my career—one that I knew would define my future as a leader. It was about more than appeasing my supervisor or satisfying the vendor. The decision I made would reflect directly on my integrity and credibility. If word ever got out, or if someone uncovered the truth, it would shape how others perceived me for years to come. I understood in that moment that my reputation, my values, and my personal brand as a leader were all on the line.

That is when it hit me. This was the moment I had to confront unethical practices and speak out against this behavior. Regardless of the professional consequences, I realized that my reputation, my brand, and my influence mattered far more than a single project. Let me tell you, this was not easy. It took courage and integrity to challenge not only the vendor, but also my immediate supervisor. But I did it, and I did not get fired. In fact, I was praised, and my decision was respected. That was the moment I stepped into my role as a leader, and it was the point where my influence began to gain real momentum and power.

I finally felt comfortable being the ethical leader I had always known I had the potential to be. It was no longer a choice; it was a decision. But how did I get here? That was something I constantly reflected on and pondered. I needed to understand the reasoning behind my decision so I could share my experience and help others facing similar challenges. That was when it finally hit me. I had inadvertently built a personal framework to help me navigate the ethical situations I would continue to encounter throughout the course of my career.

I had taken deliberate steps to lead with integrity instead of fear. I recognized my core values and beliefs and set boundaries I was unwilling to cross in the course of my professional duties. This was the crux of my decision to practice ethical leadership. It became my guiding light, giving me clarity whenever I faced a difficult decision or challenging choice. It also taught me to be critical and disciplined in my approach by using a simple, structured framework: consider the facts, evaluate the alternatives, and reflect on how each option aligns with core principles like justice, fairness, and rights. That was it, and it was simple. After putting this into practice, I made it a point to evaluate my decisions and seek feedback from peers and colleagues.

When facing difficult choices, you do not always need to go it alone. You can rely on others as trusted consultants to help you gain perspective and insight. This approach has saved me numerous times, and led to some of the best decisions of my career. I often reflect on these decisions and critically evaluate them to identify areas for improvement, continuously practicing the feedback loop that drives personal and professional growth.

Building Your Ethical Legacy

These are all important aspects of being an ethical leader in thought leadership. You must be honest and truthful, avoiding the pitfalls of exaggeration or distortion, by sticking to the facts, and the facts only. It is always important to acknowledge any potential bias or conflicts of interest that could compromise your credibility. It is best practice to be upfront with your audience rather than leaving them to question your motives or search for clarification. Always remain self-aware of the power that comes with influence. Understand that your message carries tremendous weight, and even one small error or piece of misinformation can create a dangerous ripple effect that leads to poor decisions and unintended consequences.

We must be accountable and own our mistakes. As thought leaders, we must always prioritize integrity and respect. Always cite your sources, list your methodology, and present your information accurately to your audience. Lastly, focus on the long-term impact of your decisions. Your influence goes far beyond a single speech, presentation, or meeting. Whether you realize it or not, your words and actions will have a lasting effect on others and, in many cases, on society. One of the most surprising lessons I have learned throughout my career is that, no matter how insignificant your words may feel at the moment, they almost always impact at least one person every time you speak or share your expertise.

This is the foundation you will use as a leader to build your lasting legacy. It is about more than success; it is about creating a legacy rooted in values that leave a positive impact on individuals, organizations, and ultimately your industry. As leaders, we must define the unique values that will form the cornerstone of our legacy. These non-negotiable beliefs serve as our compass, guiding our decisions, shaping our behavior, and influencing how we are remembered long after our titles and accomplishments fade.

At the core of this is your why, the connection between your personal values and a larger mission. When your values and actions align with that mission, your legacy becomes not just what you accomplish, but what you inspire others to carry forward.

To anchor this work, take the time to craft a legacy statement. This is a concise declaration of your values and purpose that keeps your behavior aligned with your vision. Remember, with influence comes responsibility. Ethics build trust. Integrity sustains credibility. In the end, your legacy will not be defined by the titles you hold, but by the values you uphold and the lives you touch.

Chapter 10

Shaping the Future: A Thought Leader's Legacy

"Carve your name on hearts, not tombstones." – Shannon L. Alder

Traditionally, when we hear the word, legacy, we think of past accomplishments or achievements that will be remembered long after we are gone. But legacy is not only about what we leave behind; it is about what we build for the future. As leaders, we must move beyond reflection and embrace forward thinking. Our role is not simply to be remembered, but to empower and equip future generations to grow, adapt, and lead with even greater purpose.

When your legacy is rooted solely in memory, it becomes a static relic—something frozen in time that risks fading into obscurity as the world evolves. True legacy, however, is dynamic. It adapts, grows, and remains relevant because it continues to live through the people, systems, and ideas you have helped shape. To move beyond mere remembrance, we must build an infrastructural legacy—one grounded in tangible, evolving systems that empower future progress and sustain the impact of our leadership long after we are gone.

But what exactly do we mean by infrastructural legacy? What does it look like in the context of thought leadership? When thought leadership intersects with infrastructure, it becomes about building systems, processes, and frameworks that outlast the individual. It is about transforming your expertise into a repeatable model or playbook that others can use, adapt, and expand. In doing so, you shift from being backward-looking, focused on what has been accomplished, to being forward-looking, creating pathways for others to build upon your work and carry your vision further into the future.

The essence of legacy infrastructure is creating a roadmap for others to follow, offering best practices and guiding principles to help them achieve the same level of success you have attained. It is, in many ways, the cheat code to your journey. For me, that legacy infrastructure is this book. I did not write it simply to capture past accomplishments, but rather to provide you with a framework—a living guide to help you navigate your own path as a thought leader, innovator, and change agent. For it to work, it needs to be fully adaptable and elastic to stand the test of time. Our goal is to provide a flexible framework that can be applied to guide decision-making, by empowering others with tools that outlast your tenure.

We discussed the power of storytelling in detail earlier in the book. This section does not replace that concept, but rather builds upon it, adding more depth and dimension to our discussion. Here, we move beyond storytelling and step into the role of a teacher, focusing on transferring knowledge, rather than relying solely on anecdotes to illustrate or emphasize a lesson. This is where we turn experience into education, ensuring that what we've learned does not end with us, but continues to shape the next generation of leaders.

Our legacy becomes tangible and enduring when it is embedded in our values and systems. This approach makes it adaptable to future change, creating a platform where others can build their success using the foundation we've established. These systems ensure that our impact continues long after we are gone, providing stability, guidance, and inspiration for those who follow.

The goal of building a long-lasting legacy is creating one that is forward-thinking and centered on continuity rather than commemoration. The focus shifts from celebrating past achievements to establishing enduring principles, systems, and values that continue to evolve and inspire future generations. In doing so, we move from being remembered for what we accomplished to being revered for what we enabled others to achieve.

Discovering this was an empowering moment for me that came later in my professional career. Initially, I believed I was building a legacy by memorializing my accomplishments on platforms like LinkedIn and Instagram. But over time, I realized it was more than establishing credibility or influence; it was about impact. I was not just building a legacy for recognition, I was creating one meant to educate, empower, and elevate others. As a thought leader, I came to understand that my responsibility extended beyond personal achievement. It was about sharing insights, experiences, and lessons learned with my industry colleagues and peers so they could grow, innovate, and lead in their own right.

I had to completely rethink what legacy building meant and shift from a monument mindset to a movement mindset. It required a fundamental change in how I viewed my purpose and how I wanted to be remembered. And to be honest, it was not easy. It demanded that I reprogram my thinking and expand my perspective. Yes, I still wanted my past accomplishments to live on after I was gone, but more importantly, I wanted to create a pathway for others to follow. My goal evolved from preserving my legacy to empowering others to build upon it, transforming it into something living, dynamic, and enduring.

These principles are grounded in the ideology of commemoration and continuity as the central tenets of our transition. When we talk about commemoration, we refer to the desire to be remembered for past accomplishments, titles, or milestones. The challenge with this approach is that when a legacy is built solely on past achievements, its longevity depends entirely on the perceived significance of those accomplishments. Once that significance fades, so does the legacy.

A perfect example of this concept is Sam Walton, the founder of Walmart. His influence and vision were so profound that his legacy continues to live on in the company's culture and identity even decades after his passing. However, since his death, Walmart has had four CEOs, and none of their legacies have carried the same lasting resonance. They are remembered in company history books, but not in the hearts of employees or the public consciousness in the same way as Walton is.

Take Lee Scott, for example. His tenure as CEO from 2000 to 2009 was marked by immense growth and global expansion, leading Walmart into new markets and significantly increasing sales. Yet, despite these remarkable achievements, his legacy is largely confined to the company's historical records. It lacks the folklore-like presence that made Sam Walton's story a part of Walmart's DNA.

This illustrates that commemoration-based legacies, while meaningful, often remain static. They honor the past, but do little to inspire the future. Continuity, on the other hand, represents the evolution of legacy. It lives, breathes, and grows through the people we develop and the systems we establish. It is about creating frameworks, cultures, and practices that outlast our tenure and empower others to succeed long after we are gone.

When we focus on continuity, our impact extends beyond recognition. It becomes a living, evolving force that adapts to new challenges and opportunities. The people we mentor, the policies we shape, and the structures we leave behind become carriers of our values and amplifiers of our vision. In this way, our legacy transforms from something that is remembered to something that continues to do—a legacy in motion.

The purpose of this section is to emphasize that legacy is not defined by a single grand achievement or moment of recognition. It is built through the compounding effect of your daily actions and the consistency of your values. Legacy is about walking the walk rather than simply talking the talk. It is about creating a clear path for others to follow and emulate. At its core, it requires self-sacrifice, the willingness to give, guide, and invest in others without the expectation of immediate return. This is when your legacy becomes more than a reflection of your success. It becomes a testament to how you lived and, more importantly, how you empowered others to live better.

Our legacy is intentionally cultivated and designed; it does not occur by accident or happen by chance. As thought leaders, we take deliberate steps each day to shape our brand and reputation. But how does this actually happen? It begins with alignment, ensuring that your actions are consistent with your core values. When what you do reflects what you believe, every decision, conversation, and contribution becomes a building block of your legacy.

Remember when we discussed vision earlier in the book? It comes into play here because it serves as the anchor for your legacy. You must have a genuine understanding of what you want to be known for and the impact you want to leave on future generations. Once your vision is clearly defined, the next step is to consistently and intentionally embody those principles and values in your behavior, both personally and professionally. This alignment between what you believe, what you say, and what you do is what transforms your vision from an abstract idea into a living legacy.

From there, it becomes your responsibility to share these insights with your community to inspire others to follow in your footsteps, provide guidance, and continue the cycle of growth. A legacy lives on when it empowers others to dream bigger, lead with purpose, and carry forward the values that define you.

"Legacy is the byproduct of leadership, not the pursuit of it."
— Dr. George J Mclean

As we step forward into the next chapter of our personal and professional journeys, let us remember that thought leadership is not a destination; it is a lifelong pursuit of growth, purpose, and service. The true measure of leadership lies not in the titles we hold or the accolades we receive, but in the lives we touch, the systems we build, and the integrity we uphold when no one is watching. Every conversation, decision, and act of courage adds another brick to the foundation of our legacy.

The world will continue to evolve, presenting new challenges and opportunities that test our resilience and vision. But if we stay grounded in our values and committed to ethical influence, we will not only adapt; we will shape the future. Let this be your call to persevere with intention, lead with authenticity, and inspire others to rise alongside you.

I want to leave you with one final message: now is the time to act; not next year, not next month, not tomorrow, but today. Begin to deliberately apply the tools, wisdom, and strategies we have explored over the past nine chapters to your real-world experiences. Take it one step at a time, and do it with intention. Remember, Rome was not built in a day, and neither will your legacy be. It is constructed through the small, consistent actions and behaviors you exhibit every single day.

I have probably said this ten times by now, but it bears repeating: walk the walk, do not just talk the talk. Wear your values on your sleeve, boldly, authentically, and unapologetically. Chart the path forward, so that others can emulate your success and learn from your example. One of the most effective ways to do this is by becoming a mentor, teaching courses, or writing blogs, books, and articles. Personally, I have found all three to be powerful avenues to express and embody my values within my industry, ensuring that what I believe in continues to shape and inspire others long after the conversation ends.

Start today. Lead one person. Share one lesson. Stand by one principle when it is easier to stay silent. Each act, no matter how small, leaves a mark that someone else will carry forward. Legacies are built by one intentional choice, one moment of courage, and one act of purpose at a time.

Before we close, take a moment to define your legacy in your own words. Write it down, revisit it, and refine it as you grow. This is your final **Pause and Reflect Exercise**, designed to help you connect all the dots and paint the bigger picture of your leadership journey.

Pause and Reflect Exercise

Take a few minutes to write down your honest answers to the following questions:

- My purpose is to...
- I will live my values by...
- The impact I want to leave behind is...
- My legacy will live on through...

Once you complete this, save it and turn it into your **Legacy Statement**. This is more than just a statement; it is your personal credo. It will evolve with you as your leadership and values grow. Think of it as part of your feedback loop—a living reflection of your growth and self-awareness.

I encourage you to revisit it periodically, reflect on your progress, and update it as you evolve toward the best version of yourself—one that fully aligns with your core values.

Remember the exercise we discussed earlier about gauging alignment? It is simple: ask a trusted friend or colleague to describe you in three words. If those words align with how you want your personal brand and legacy to be perceived, you are on the right track—keep going. If they do not, enter the feedback loop, recalibrate, and move forward with purpose.

Your legacy is not written once; it is lived, refined, and strengthened through the choices you make every day. This is a monumental step in your journey, and I am glad that you have decided to take the first step towards becoming a credible leader. Remember, this journey is not a sprint; it is a marathon. You have to make daily strides towards becoming the best version of yourself and a better leader. Reading this book and making it this far is a huge step, and shows your commitment to growth.

Take a moment to celebrate, but do not stop. This transition into becoming a true thought leader is both challenging and deeply rewarding. You will experience many ups and downs along the way. There will be moments when you achieve something significant, yet the recognition or celebration from others may never come. That is normal, and it is okay.

This journey goes far deeper than a social media post or public acknowledgment. You are stepping into your light as a professional and as a leader in your industry. The courage to learn, the humility to grow, and the wisdom to guide others are the true marks of leadership.

The goal of this book has been to serve as your compass—a guide you can return to whenever the path feels uncertain. Let it remind you of who you are, what you stand for, and the purpose that drives your perseverance. You are not just shaping your future; you are shaping the future.

CONCLUSION

As our journey comes to an end, it is important to reflect on the new ideals we have discussed over the past ten chapters that have brought us to this point. This text was originally rooted in expanding your touchpoints as a leader, sharpening your thinking, and challenging you to approach your work with greater clarity, purpose, and influence. What began as a collection of lessons from years of experience evolved into a framework designed to help you grow, adapt, and lead with confidence in an ever-changing world.

Throughout these chapters, we explored the power of perseverance, the responsibility of credibility, and the importance of consistent action. We examined how thought leadership is shaped through intentional practice, how innovation fuels relevance, and how ethical influence forms the foundation of long-term success. Each idea was crafted to support your development, both in mindset and in application, ensuring that the principles presented here can serve as a guide well beyond the pages of this book.

My hope is that this text has encouraged you to think differently about your potential, your role, your relationships, and the impact you are capable of making. Leadership is not defined by position. It is defined by how you show up, how you communicate, and how you choose to add value in every environment you enter.

As you step forward, carry these insights with you. Continue refining your craft. Seek challenges that push you to grow. Lead with integrity, humility, and determination. And remember that influence is not built in a moment; it is earned through daily actions, intentional decisions, and a commitment to excellence.

Thank you for walking this journey with me. May these lessons support you as you build your legacy, elevate your

AUTHOR'S NOTE

Thank you for choosing to spend your time with this book. Completing a journey like this requires intention, refection, and a real commitment to growth qualities that define credible leadership. I do not take that lightly.

This book was written with leaders like you in mind. Leaders who care deeply about doing meaningful work, serving with integrity, and leaving the world better because they showed up. My hope is that these pages challenged you to think differently, encouraged you to lean into your authenticity, and reminded you that leadership is not about perfection but about purpose.

As you move forward know that you are not alone on this journey. Each lesson you apply, each person you mentor, and each courageous decision you make adds another chapter to the leadership legacy you are building.

Thank you for walking this path with me.

Dr. George J. Mclean
Author, Educator, and Thought Leader

ABOUT THE AUTHOR

Dr. George J. McLean is a leadership strategist, educator, and author whose work focuses on bridging the gap between knowledge, influence, and practical action. With a career spanning more than fifteen years across business, analytics, operations, and organizational development, he has built a reputation for helping leaders think with clarity, act with intention, and drive meaningful results.

Dr. McLean's professional journey blends experience in complex public-sector environments with a deep commitment to strategic planning, data-driven decision-making, and ethical leadership. His contributions include developing high-impact initiatives, advising executive teams, and leading multidisciplinary projects centered on innovation, governance, and organizational excellence.

As an adjunct professor of American Government, he is passionate about teaching, mentoring, and helping students build the confidence and discipline needed to succeed academically and professionally. His work in both the classroom and executive settings reflects a belief that leadership is not defined by titles, but by integrity, consistency, and the willingness to grow.

Dr. McLean holds advanced degrees in business and public administration, along with specialized training in leadership and management. He continues to speak, write, and consult on topics related to strategic leadership, credibility, and the future of work.

He is driven by a simple mission: to empower others to lead with purpose, elevate their influence, and create lasting impact in the communities and organizations they serve.

www.ingramcontent.com/pod-product-compliance
Lightning Source LLC
Chambersburg PA
CBHW020333010526
44119CB00002B/51